THE WORKPLACE BULLYING HANDBOOK

How to Identify, Prevent,
and Stop a Workplace Bully

I work in the communications industry with clients from all sectors of industry and government. Paul's book encapsulates what our clients have been asking for: an easy-to-read manual with common sense approaches that effectively and strategically confront workplace bullies. Paul has provided training and presentations to many of our clients. The combination of this handbook and Paul's gift for inspiring people to take action makes an important contribution to this field.

—Amy Ruddell,
Senior Director, Macgregor Communications, and
editor-in-chief of *ProjectTimes*, Toronto, Canada

The genius of this book is its location in the everyday experiences and examples with its practical applications to extremely complex issues. A must read for anyone in the contemporary workplace.

—Dr. Blye Frank,
Dean of the Faculty of Education,
University of British Columbia, Canada

Paul Pelletier extends his expertise and knowledge about how to prevent and fight workplace bullying, making the office a safe area where people can develop their best potential. Paul provides a set of concrete and tangible actions and tools to operationalize the management of workplace bullies. Essential reading for any manger motivated to sustain and develop their businesses.

—Olivier Lazar,
Managing Partner & COO,
The Valense Palatine Group, Geneva, Switzerland

I encourage anyone in a leadership role to take the time to read Paul's highly insightful book. This is such an important topic that often lurks beneath the surface at many organizations, quietly eroding the success of a company. Paul uses his personal and professional experiences to help provide perspective on the significant impact bullying can have in a workplace. In addition, Paul provides clear and concise tools to help organizations not only identify and address concerning behavior, but also suggestions on how to ensure leaders are "walking the walk" and promoting a culture where everyone truly feels safe and is treated with respect and dignity.

—Tracy Torrell CPHR,
Human Resources Manager,
Hollyburn Properties Limited, Vancouver, Canada

ISBN print: 978-0-9950036-2-0
ISBN ebook: 978-0-9950036-3-7

Cover design by Linda Parke
           Raven Book Design
Book design by Patti Frazee and Levi Satterlee

Disclaimer

It is important to note that the advice and examples in this book are intended as a guide only. The contents of this book do not constitute legal advice and aren't a substitute for specific legal advice or opinions. It may be appropriate to seek the help of professionals (legal, health care, human resources, consultants, and others) depending on the nature of the situation.

All the stories in this book are real. Further, the examples may resemble other people's bullying situations because many bullies exhibit similar behaviors. Such resemblance is purely coincidental. Names used have been changed and have no reference to real persons. Organizations are not revealed in respect of their privacy, except in the context of other published material in which they have been named.

Finally, the opinions within this book are those of the author's alone and don't represent the opinions of any organization or the publisher.

The information provided herein is stated to be truthful and consistent, in that any liability, in terms of inattention or otherwise, by use or abuse of any policies, processes, or directions contained within is the solitary and utter responsibility of the recipient reader. Under no circumstance will any legal responsibility or blame be held against the publisher or author for any reparation, damages, or monetary loss due to the information herein, either directly or indirectly.

Published by
Diversity Publishing
Vancouver, Canada

Table of Contents

Acknowledgments

The beginning is the most important part of the work.

—Plato

It's been two years since I wrote my first book on workplace bullying. I could never had known that the process of writing *Workplace Bullying: It's Just Bad for Business* would lead to so many opportunities to increase awareness and help others confronting bullies at work.

Since then, I've had the privilege of working with many organizations addressing workplace respect and bullying challenges. Whether it's speaking at a conference, in a workshop or webinar, in a training session for staff or sitting around a boardroom table, people discuss their experiences. I want to thank all the courageous people who have shared their stories about workplace bullying, harassment, and other forms of workplace disrespect. I also thank the executives and organizational leaders who are engaging directly and implementing zero-tolerance policies and effective processes to ensure there are no bullies in their ranks. You've all enlightened me and provoked me to conclude there is a need for a workplace bullying handbook.

As a frequent presenter at conferences and workshops, I'm constantly reminded that the bullying experience I thought I was enduring in silence is actually one that thousands of others relate to. I'm also aware that as you read this book, there are thousands of people who are currently being impacted by workplace bullies and harassers. You are the inspiration for this book. It is my sincere hope that, together, we will become better informed and empowered to take action to raise awareness, effectively address our bullies, and create a global policy of zero tolerance for bullying in our workplaces.

To those who continue to support me in this unexpected personal and professional journey, I owe much gratitude. From a traditional career in the legal and business world to an advocate against workplace bullying – thank you for encouraging me to remain focused in the pursuit of a higher purpose.

To my editor Patti Frazee – thank you for your wisdom and guidance. You've managed to turn a lawyer into a book writer. I'm sure that wasn't easy!

To my friends and family who suffered while I was in the midst of the bullying hurricane and supported me through the fallout and re-building process – thank you for your patience, compassion, and guidance. From you I learned that my experience could be used to not only heal myself but also help others who find themselves in a similar predicament.

To the medical professionals who cared for me and helped me heal both physically and mentally – you gave me back my health and passion to take the bully and organization supporting him to task. Despite the odds and result, I firmly believe that we have a choice to be powerless or face our fears head-on.

I've engaged with people around the world – it is an irrefutable fact that workplace bullying is a global challenge across all sectors. While I believe things are improving, the only way that the status quo can change is if enough of us decide to take action. As a society, we need to disrupt the system that supports and, all too often, protects the bullies and harassers.

In effect, we need to start a #MeToo movement for workplace bullying. I'm well aware that we won't change the world instantly, but like the #MeToo movement, we can progress far beyond a hashtag. As each of us learn skills to take action and put those skills into action, the impact of our actions reverberates beyond us, representing the "disruption movement" that I believe is necessary for change. With that higher purpose and hope for the future, I find inspiration from others much wiser than I.

This book is dedicated to the one person who held me up and continues to inspire me to keep going. You keep me honest and make me a better man every day.

THE WORKPLACE BULLYING HANDBOOK

How to Identify, Prevent, and Stop a Workplace Bully

Paul Pelletier, LL.B. PMP

Introduction

Everyone … likely has a bullying story, whether as the victim, bully, or as a witness.
—Michael M. Honda[1]

Fifteen years ago, the word "bullying" was a word used almost exclusively in the context of our schools and the suffering of children at the hands of cruel classmates. The world has awakened to the reality of this behavior in broader contexts. We now hear about bullying almost every day, still in our schools and on the Internet, but with rapidly growing regularity in our workplaces.

We also hear about it in the broader context of workplace respect and through the workplace respect policies that many of our organizations establish. Finally, in more recent news, we are seeing a rash of high-profile cases of workplace bullying, sexual harassment, and other disrespectful behavior that spawned a great deal of both media and public interest. Sadly, we are still seeing organizations promoting bullies and, in particularly disturbing circumstances, people electing bullies as their leaders. I see these situations as great opportunities for the world to witness first-hand the chaos, disrespect, and dysfunction caused by a workplace bully. It opens the door to new awareness and, I believe, a motivational wake-up call.

Bullying in the workplace is a significant global problem that, just like cancer or economics, ignores the borders of culture, nationality, gender, class, age, or other traditional distinction. It not only causes harm to those in the target zone of the bullies but also enormous negative impacts to the workplace culture, projects, programs, profits, and success of our organizations.

I challenge you to Google "workplace bullying" as a starting point. There is a plethora of useful articles, research papers, stories, and websites dedicated to the topic, and there's even a Workplace Bullying Institute. The United Kingdom has a National Workplace Bullying Advice Line. As one US TV newscast described it, the "dirty little workplace secret" of workplace bullying is now being fully exposed.

It may also come as a surprise to know that there are many YouTube videos about workplace bullying – everything from TED Talks[2] to TV news and journalistic essays on the topic. In short, there is an abundance of useful and readily available information, research, and tools for preventing, identifying, and addressing workplace bullying.

However, many of us (including me) find this abundance of information overwhelming, particularly when we are stressed because we are dealing with a challenging person at work. We need an easy-to-read, practical handbook – a single resource that focuses exclusively on the lessons learned from experience and practical tips for where to begin when we are confronted with a potential bullying problem. That is the inspiration for this book. By bringing together my personal experience, the experiences of hundreds of others that have been shared with me, and the most salient bits of research and information available, I hope that this handbook fills a much-needed void.

I believe we need this handbook because, despite the wealth of data and reasons why organizations should take action to eliminate bullying, they rarely do. All too often, they have fostered, promoted, supported and, ultimately, protected the bully. They do this for a variety of reasons, but one of the most common is that bullies are adept task masters that can "whip a unit into shape" or "get that project done." Organizations ignore the means that bullies use to achieve the ends that matter most to them – the results. In effect, they know that people are being treated badly, but the short-term results trump the personal and workplace-culture harm that bullies cause. In blunt terms, the benefits outweigh the costs as seen from the eyes of organizational leaders.

As long as organizations believe the results that bullies achieve are more important than a respectful work environment and health of their employees, the power will remain in favor of bullies. Therein lies the biggest challenge we face to confront and eliminate workplace bullying – convincing our organizations and societies around the world that the problems, financial impact, and risks that bullies create are far more serious and long-term than any "positive" short-term results that a bully achieves.

Even when our organizations either decide to address the problem or are forced to take action to deal with a workplace bully (i.e., because of a formal investigation, a threatened or actual lawsuit, a public relations problem, a workplace culture crisis), the actions taken often prove ineffective. In fact, in many cases, organizations end up making matters worse, causing even greater harm to those who are impacted or being victimized. Usually this happens because our organizations don't understand workplace bullying and what's going on. Our organizations and human resource professionals don't have the proper perspective, policies, resources, or courage to confront the problem head-on.

Organizations frequently treat a bullying situation like any other workplace conflict. This approach never works because they are totally different problems. Organizations are also afraid to deal with the "Tasmanian Devil," "Queen Bee," "Control Freak," or "Workplace Terrorist" (all terms I've heard used to describe bullies) because they know it will be ugly, unpleasant, and risky. They rarely bring in objective experts to investigate in a fair and unbiased process – this would be an acknowledgment that there is a problem, and they fear the floodgates of reported incidents will open. Finally, they regularly don't follow their own workplace respect policies. For all of these reasons, bullies often are given a "get out of jail free" card that no one else gets. And, thus, the bullying continues.

With organizations failing to stop bullying, governments are taking on the issue. Many countries have acknowledged that workplace bullying poses a health risk to workers, and most of the Western world has enacted anti-bullying legislation to protect workers. These laws have led the charge to force organizations to implement training and programs to address workplace bullying.

This book is dedicated to enhancing awareness of workplace bullying and the range of diabolical impacts it creates for people and organizations. I also hope to empower those who face bullying directly – the victims (commonly called a "target" in the context of workplace bullying), coworkers, managers, and executives. Most of us lack the skills or information to objectively identify and appreciate the motivation behind workplace bullying. By providing useful and non-judgmental information, tips, and tools, everyone will be better able to not simply cope, but to take action to address our workplace bullies.

The good news is that increased public awareness, recent research, and expanding illegalization of workplace bullying have paved the way for efforts to prevent it and eliminate it. Both employees and their employers are becoming more acutely aware of the impacts and costs associated with bullying. Bullying thrives in silence, with targets and coworkers feeling too intimidated or with too much at risk for them to confront the bully or complain.

If managers, human resources personnel, and senior level executives take initiative in addressing bullying early on, much larger financial, ethical, legal, stakeholder, and project problems will be avoided. Eventually, it is my hope that these initiatives will lead to wider support for zero tolerance for bullying in the workplace regardless of circumstance, societal norm, or jurisdiction.

1

The Anatomy of Bullying

The time is always right to do what is right.
—Martin Luther King[3]

Bullying can be as harmful in the workplace as it is in schools and other areas of society, causing the well-understood emotional and physical impacts, plus a long list of challenges for employees and their organizations. More sobering are the clear and irrefutable statistics – workplace bullying is costing businesses billions of dollars annually. For every short-term result that a bully achieves, there is a list of longer-term negative business impacts that far outweigh any temporary benefits. To quote Patricia Barnes, a workplace bullying author, judge, and attorney, workplace bullying is likely the "single most preventable and needless expense on a company's register."[4]

A conversation about bullying should start with recognition of the ethical and leadership dilemma it creates. Hopefully, we all agree that supporting, condoning, or fostering bullying is unethical and not "what is right." I have faith that the vast majority of us have a moral compass that directs us to immediately conclude that bullying and harassment of any sort is just plain wrong. You wouldn't be reading this book if you disagreed with this perspective.

Further, I assume that we also accept that bullying isn't a positive, effective, or ethical leadership style. Authoritarian and fear-based leadership might work on a battlefield, but our workplaces aren't war zones. Employees shouldn't be diagnosed with post-traumatic stress or have regularly occurring nightmares from treatment they received from a colleague at work. Going to work under a cloak of fear, chaos, and dysfunction caused by a bully leader is incompatible with the concept of good business practices.

It is a well-understood leadership principal that ethical behavior is part of an essential foundation for trust that we all must earn in order to succeed. This is not only my opinion – this perspective has been underscored by some of the most important thought leaders of our time. *The Leadership Challenge* by Kouzes and Posner is the gold standard for research-based leadership and is a premier resource for aspiring leaders. The text informs us that leadership requires trust:

> *It's clear that if people anywhere are to willingly follow someone – whether it be into battle or into the boardroom, the front office or the front lines – they first want to assure themselves that the person is worthy of their trust.*[5]

All our work is, for the most part, an activity undertaken in concert with others. While we may refer to these others as team members, stakeholders, or coworkers, we depend on them for the success of our organizations. If employees don't trust or feel supported by their leaders, there will be no motivation or commitment to fully engage.

Following this logic and with many scholars and research in support, without ethical leadership (which includes sincerely and effectively responding to bullying) there will be few fully engaged and high-performance teams, and even fewer program, project, and innovation successes. Think of the organizational impacts that flow from this conclusion. Put simply, an organization whose leaders are bullies or whose leaders support the bad behavior of bullies working under them is an unethical organization with unethical leaders.

We've seen a significant increase in public awareness about ethics in our organizations and leaders. Sadly, much of the awareness has come through reports and investigations into globally significant organizations that have made extraordinarily bad ethical and leadership decisions (Volkswagen, Uber, Facebook, Wells Fargo, Samsung, and Miramax, to name a few). It has often taken years of abuse and well-known unethical behavior before the truth comes out (or, more importantly, these organizations and their executives have been caught and held accountable).

The most disturbing part of these stories is that almost all of the organizations have workplace respect, ethical behavior, and anti-harassment policies that are designed to ensure a safe, respectful, bully-free, harassment-free, and ethical workplace. Further, these policies supposedly protect employees from any inappropriate behavior that violates the rules. Staff are told they should report all bad behavior and they are promised that something will be done, the policy will be enforced, the culprits will be held accountable, and those who report the problem will be protected from retaliation.

Nevertheless – the experience for thousands of employees is that these policies rarely protect them. They are often unfairly and inconsistently enforced. Executives, human resources, and their legal counsel go into risk management mode, trying to protect their organization as opposed to the people who reported the problem. All too often, this results in bullies and unethical staff being the ones who receive protection.

Organizations will even go to great lengths to ensure the problem is "managed," including paying victims/

complainants to quietly leave the organization with a legal agreement binding them to never discuss the problem or settlement (often referred to as "hush money"). The short-sightedness of these responses to legitimate reports of workplace disrespect is remarkable and contrary to all ethical and business best practices.

Despite this historical trend, I believe there are signs of hope and opportunities to disrupt the status quo. For example, we've experienced a global shift in awareness and perspective on workplace harassment. Thanks to things like the #MeToo movement and the efforts of many courageous people, our organizations (and, hopefully, the broader society) are starting to take note. Traditional media and social media have put a lot of pressure on organizations to take action. In high profile cases, particularly in the entertainment, technology, and media sectors, it has resulted in some very public figures losing their jobs, careers, companies, and reputations.

It's easy to say that this reaction to public pressure is both too little and far too late. Skeptics fairly note that the organizations in question were acutely aware their staff were being abused, sometimes for years or even decades. We've also learned that because of power imbalances, politics, and risk management strategies, the bullies, harassers, and badly behaved are often protected. In the worst cases, the CEOs or senior executives running the company are the bullies. In most cases, instead of confronting the problem, organizations terminate or move impacted staff, or ignore the issue through willful blindness.

Nevertheless, I believe that from these seeds of increased awareness sprouts hope that it will lead to real change. We have to be realistic and appreciate that it often takes years for these seeds to bear fruit. However, a movement for change has begun. We all can play our part and become respectful workplace leaders and colleagues. We can "walk the walk," managing our own behavior and courageously responding when we see others behave badly.

We can take an active role in participating in the movement to eliminate workplace bullying. It won't be easy or enjoyable but it is the right thing to do – for you, for your coworkers, for your workplace, and for society.

What Is Workplace Bullying?

Knowledge is power. Information is liberating. Education is the premise of progress, in every society, in every family.

—Kofi Annan,
Former Secretary-General of the United Nations[6]

From this place of hope, and with an enhanced appreciation that bullying is unethical and creating preventable negative impacts on our organizations, we can begin to study the behaviors of bullies. We can also create strategies for identifying and addressing bullying in our workplaces.

As strange as it seems, one of the most-asked questions I get is: "What exactly *is* workplace bullying?" This is entirely understandable because, as of the date of publication of this book, there is still no definition for "workplace bullying" in *Merriam Webster's Dictionary*.[7] There is a definition of "bullying" that includes all contexts of "abuse and mistreatment of someone vulnerable by someone stronger, more powerful, etc." This definition doesn't adequately describe or differentiate a workplace bully from a schoolyard bully. With all the research and discussion about workplace bullying, it seems unfathomable that there isn't a proper definition for this term, especially considering terms can be found such as "pleather," "sexting," "LOL," and other contemporary words.

After I gave a presentation on workplace bullying, a woman approached me in tears. She always wondered what was going on with her boss, but she simply couldn't place her finger on a proper identifier for the daily attacks she was facing. It wasn't until she saw a definition of "workplace bullying" that it became clear. The more examples of bullying behavior she heard, the more emotional she became. She told me the presentation lifted a massive weight off her – simply because she now had the right label to call her bullying boss. He wasn't just "mean," "spiteful," "disrespectful," or "unlikeable" – he was a workplace bully.

Given the lack of agreement on a common definition, we must rely on other sources to define workplace bullying. Fortunately, there are a number of highly respected and internationally renowned psychologists, professors, authors, and researchers on the subject, including Professor Ståle Einarsen (University of Bergen, Norway), Clare Rayner, Lyn Quine (University of Canterbury, UK), and Professor Sir Carey Lyne Cooper (University of Manchester, UK) to name a few. According to Einarsen, bullying at work means:

> ... *harassing, offending, socially excluding someone or negatively affecting someone's work tasks. In order for the label bullying (or mobbing) to be applied to a particular activity, interaction, or process it has to occur repeatedly and regularly (e.g. weekly) and over a period of time (e.g. about six months). Bullying is an escalated process in the course of which the person confronted ends up in an inferior position and becomes the target of systematic negative social acts.*[8]

For those who appreciate a more concise definition, the Workplace Bullying Institute defines workplace bullying as:

> *Repeated, health-harming mistreatment, verbal abuse, or conduct which is threatening, humiliating, intimidating, or sabotage that*

interferes with work, or some combination of the three.[9]

Workplace bullying is mistreatment, perpetrated by an employee, severe enough to compromise a targeted worker's health, jeopardize her or his job and career, and strain relationships with friends and family. It is deliberate, repetitive, disrespectful behavior that is always for the bully's benefit. It is a focused, systematic campaign of interpersonal destruction. All bullying can be categorized as a form of abuse. In the bluntest of terms, it is workplace terrorism.

It is important to distinguish bullying from the inappropriate, one-time acts of someone who is under a great deal of pressure, having a particularly (and unusually) bad day or handling a disagreement poorly. It could also be a situation where a combination of poor communication skills, a lack of cultural awareness, or a lack of boundaries results in bad behavior, unfortunate language choices, or regrettable conflict management tactics. These circumstances lead to behavior such as an insensitive joke, an invasion of personal space, or inappropriate things said in the heat of a moment of lost patience, frustration, or anger.

These are single events, not a pattern. They arise from a unique situation that is easy to identify. The offenders, once they have a moment to calm down, reflect, or be informed of their gaffe, appreciate they have hurt another or acted inappropriately. They understand they have breached respectful workplace behavioral expectations. Always, they are embarrassed and, almost always, they quickly and sincerely apologize. They hold themselves accountable for their actions. They show authentic remorse and the behavior is likely never repeated. The important distinction is that they have a sense of self-awareness, integrity, and morality. They course-correct and care about those they work with.

A bully's actions, on the other hand, are repetitive, intentional, and deviant. The disrespect is often planned and those with power or influence around the bully are manipulated to ensure the planned attacks will appear to them as appropriate "performance management steps," "getting the job done," or "taking care of business."

Bullies also discriminate – they target those they perceive as a threat. Their targets aren't vulnerable in the same way that a schoolyard bully attacks the weak or defenseless. As you'll see, targets may be anyone who is perceived as a threat regardless of their position.

Also, there is never only one event. The behavior of a workplace bully is an escalating series of events, a well-planned strategy to undermine and harm their victims. When confronted or questioned, bullies are adept at deflecting accountability and defending their actions. They will use the relationships that they have fostered with those above them to shield themselves. Normal conflict resolution approaches fail because these aren't normal conflicts. In fact, there is nothing "normal" about them.

Finally, bullies don't think like we do. They can't be reasoned with. They have a narcissistic, warped view of the world. Their approach to conflict is to fight to the finish using all measures to blame others, defend their actions, lie, and breach any rules that stand in their way. As we continue to see almost daily in the news, bullies don't believe the rules apply to them, even if those rules are laws.

As previously noted, in many Western jurisdictions bullying is recognized as a form of workplace violence and a hazard to workers' health. For example, the United States Department of Labor, National Institute of Occupation Safety and Health Administration's definition of "Workplace Violence" incorporates many of the foundational characteristics of bullying, including:

Any act or threat of physical violence, harassment, intimidation, or other threatening disruptive behavior that occurs at the work site.[10]

One of the difficult aspects of bullying that many find hard to grasp is that it has nothing to do with work itself. It is driven by the bully's personal agenda, based on a warped perception of who they find threatening. To complicate matters, workplace bullies are sometimes hard to clearly identify. They can be highly skilled and smart, yet socially manipulative, targeting "weaker" employees while adept at charming those they deem will serve their career path well. Bullies are usually focused on achieving results, regardless of means, ethics, or fairness. Sadly, it is often those results that senior managers are impressed with and focus on.

Overlooking the staff turnover, absences, team dysfunction, and low employee engagement levels, there are many stories where the bully's senior manager or supervisor says, "John seems great to me." Often, the higher-ups are well aware that John really is a bully, but instead describe him as "difficult," "runs a tight ship," "hard to get along with," or that he "suffers no fools." They ignore what they know deep down is bullying, because the short-term results trump the other considerations.

Bullies also create a real-life *Devil Wears Prada*[11] situation where everyone except those who work for the bully both fear and revere her at the same time. For outsiders, she is a symbol of the pinnacle of achievement or an iconic visionary. However, they also know that she is a force best not confronted, and that you never want to be on her bad side or "hit list." Those underneath her are ruled by intimidation, workplace terrorism, and appallingly unreasonable expectations. Driven by their insatiable egos, bullies see compassion, kindness, and fairness as weakness. In some cases, their narcissistic personalities prevent them from feeling compassion or empathy at all. They're always in defense mode, deflecting blame away from themselves and lying to cover their tracks. The workplace is their battlefield and for them, the winner takes all.

Typical Bullying Behaviors

I have no right, by anything I do or say, to demean a human being in his own eyes. What matters is not what I think of him; it is what he thinks of himself. To undermine a man's self-respect is a sin.

—Antoine de Saint-Exupery[12]

Bullies play by a simple zero-sum game mentality – the bullies see that their targets have something the bullies don't, and they will do whatever they need to in order to secure that "something" or take it away. In the process, they may destroy the target as well. I have heard hundreds of stories about workplace bullying from every sector, profession, culture, and type of organization and corner of the world. There are threads of behavior that wind through most bullying stories. While each bully adopts their own form of workplace terrorism, bullying usually includes behaviors that can be categorized into three types, as outlined below (this is a list of representative examples and isn't exhaustive):

Aggressive Communication
- Eye rolling, intentionally interrupting, shutting down conversations
- Insulting or making offensive remarks
- Shouting, yelling, angry outbursts
- Using their bodies and body language as weapons to intimidate (i.e. standing over others, crossing their arms aggressively)
- Breaching commonly understood boundaries (i.e. in-

vading personal space, using unprofessional language, making inappropriate requests to fudge or ignore organizational policies, harassing others)

- Going around coworkers in order to avoid communicating with them
- Saying something inappropriate and then immediately taking it back or unauthentically apologizing (i.e., "it was just a joke.")
- Using meetings and other group settings to embarrass, single out, or humiliate others
- Harsh finger-pointing, shoving, blocking the way
- Staring others down, giving dirty looks
- Sending angry emails or other e-communications (often using exclamation points, bold lettering, and underlining to create a harsh tone or stress)
- Copying others in an email that berates or criticizes their target
- Humiliating or ridiculing, excessive teasing
- Spreading rumors or gossip that they know aren't true
- Ignoring peers when they walk by
- Playing harsh practical jokes
- Taunting with the use of social media

Manipulation of Work
- Removing tasks imperative to job responsibilities
- Giving unmanageable workloads & impossible deadlines
- Arbitrarily changing tasks
- Using employee evaluations to document supposed poor work quality without setting goals or providing the tools needed to improve

Sabotaging Work
- Hinting that someone should quit, nobody likes him

or her, or the boss thinks they are incompetent

- Withholding pertinent information needed to do one's job effectively
- Leaving employees out of communication loops
- Excessive micromanagement (commonly called the "control freaks")
- Failing to give credit, or stealing credit for others' work
- Preventing access to opportunities like promotions or raises
- Consistently pointing out mistakes, however little or long ago they occurred

***

Combining the requirements for repetition, deliberateness, and disrespectfulness with this list of behaviors usually results in the successful identification of a bully (or not). Bullying isn't a personality clash or a relationship conflict – it is pathological, abusive behavior that can be identified.

What Isn't Workplace Bullying?

For good idea and true innovation, you need human interaction, conflict, argument, debate.

—Margaret Heffernan, Businesswoman[13]

Not every unpleasant or challenging conflict with people at work or in a project is bullying. On the contrary, conflict is a normal part of life and, as you may know too well, conflict in our pressure- and deadline-filled workplaces is a regular occurrence. So, it's important to contrast normal work behavior and interaction, particularly in uncomfortable and difficult times, from bullying.

For example, Sebastian shared his problems about a workplace relationship with a coworker. He works in the field of healthcare in a hospital surrounded by doctors, health crises, stressed-out families, sick patients, and focused healthcare workers. Everyone has his or her own agendas, concerns, and pressures. His work environment is stress-filled, ego-oriented, and decisions are made under pressure with life-and-death implications.

Sebastian described an ongoing battle with Kim, his coworker. As I heard him talking about their differences of opinion, opposing views on how to manage patients, and blow-ups in the emergency room, it was apparent to me that their conflict wasn't a bullying problem. It was a case of two professionals with strong and divergent opinions trying to achieve the same goal – improving patient results. They fought over small decisions. Kim wasn't picking on him every day. She wasn't humiliating him or sabotaging his work. The worst fights happened in stressful patient crises. This was a case of normal workplace conflict. Kim wasn't a bully. Kim and Sebastian needed to sit down, reason out their differences, and develop a respectful relationship. They had a communication breakdown that, over time, evolved into a relationship built on distrust, uncooperativeness, and disdain.

Here are some helpful examples of reasonable and regular conflicts that take place at work that wouldn't qualify as bullying, unless they also involved the behaviors noted in the definition of bullying:

Respectfully expressing differences of opinion.
Heated debates about divergent views on how to approach or resolve a challenge are normal. Many organizations purposefully encourage brainstorming sessions seeking all points of view on a particular problem. It is through active debate that we often find ways to innovate. Challenging each other's opinions is standard behavior in competitive and

high-performance team environments. It is a fundamental principal of work environments in which many of us work.

I believe these conversations are healthy and should be encouraged as they ensure that all opinions are considered. The conversations also help us grow and develop as adults. We learn humility, to open our minds to new perspectives, to embrace diversity. Conversations like this improve workplace culture and engagement.

Having to defend your position might be uncomfortable but it isn't inappropriate unless you are being humiliated and diminished in the process. We know when the line of disrespect has been crossed. The second that we feel belittled for sharing our view or when a colleague rolls her eyes when it's your turn to speak, disrespect is taking place.

I've already noted the vast difference between a single issue of impatience, ignorance, intolerance, or disrespectful behavior and a pattern of bullying. It's when there is disrespect *every time* you speak or only *when* you speak (and not when your colleagues speak) that the flag should be raised that there's a potential workplace bully.

Normal workplace conflicts

There are many reasons why people don't get along at work (or in relationships of all kinds) and end up in some form of conflict. Some of the most common conflict triggers include communication barriers, misunderstandings, miscommunications, a lack of diversity awareness, inappropriate boundaries, high-stress work situations, mental illness, forms of addiction, stereotyping, poor social skills, and differences of opinion. There are many others that I've not mentioned. All of them can easily lead to people in conflict or disagreement. This isn't bullying unless there is bullying behavior involved.

It's also useful to step back when you encounter workplace conflict to assess whether you work in a well-managed functional organization, a dysfunctional organization run by sociopathic executives, or someplace in between. Being brutally objective when you conduct this review will assist in determining how to approach the conflicts in front of you.

For example, if I'd have been more honest about the general workplace culture and who was running my bully's organization, I would quickly have realized that I was working in a seriously mismanaged, fear-based workplace. A general sense of hopelessness, misery, and vulnerability permeated the culture. People expected the worst from their leaders and managers (with good reason). It is little wonder that a bully would thrive in such a place.

Further, it would have been obvious that my workplace wouldn't handle conflicts well. Had I been able to see reality and understand the underlying power issues, I would have been better prepared for the predictable behaviors/responses that aligned with the inherent organizational dysfunction. I would also have taken a different approach to the problem and avoided many mistakes – in short, I would have devised a much different action plan and likely had more success.

If, however, when you assess your organization you conclude that it is generally ethical, well-managed, and functional, then it is fair to have faith that it will approach conflict from a balanced perspective. You should be able to work through the conflict starting from a mutually understood point of graciousness, emotional maturity, and humility.

Having managed teams comprised of individuals from wildly diverse backgrounds and perspectives, one of the hardest lessons to teach people is to appreciate that a conflict isn't about right/wrong or winning/losing. There is no "right," rather, there is a business problem (which may also be a personal/relationship problem) that needs to be solved and each of us has differing views about how to do that.

There is absolutely nothing wrong with conflict itself. In fact, it's a normal component of human interaction. Thought leaders believe that conflict is essential for innovation and that expressing differences of opinion leads to better decisions. Furthermore, effectively managing conflict is an important skill to learn in order to be successful in our careers and in life itself. The problem is that conflict takes time, work, and isn't fun.

Conflict is uncomfortable, stressful, and challenging. That doesn't make it "bad." It's simply part of life. Dealing with people who are different, difficult, stressed, or don't share our perspectives won't be easy – but we must do it. We are all accountable for developing ways to effectively and maturely handle conflict. We all have a positive responsibility to engage with our colleagues, even when that creates conflict.

I've seen an ineffective pattern of a lack of accountability in relation to conflicts in many workplaces. This pattern leads to most of us doing whatever we can to avoid it, even though we know, deep down, that such avoidance will never serve us well. I've tried to inspire others to confront their natural tendency to avoid conflict. One tactic with which I've had some success is asking those involved in conflict one question: "What value are you bringing to the team or organization if you avoid some of the most important conversations to creatively problem solve because there is some conflict in those conversations?"

Unfortunately, logic isn't usually what's driving the avoidance – the elephant in the room is fear. We are afraid of confronting those with whom we have a conflict. Instead of working out why we disagree, we run for the hills when it hits. This fear-based perspective on conflict leads to many unfortunate workplace misunderstandings and unnecessary stress. It also leads to bad decisions and failures.

The key with conflict is that, as long as it's managed respectfully, it isn't bad or part of a pattern of bullying. My conflict mantra is: "We can agree to disagree without being disrespectful or disagreeable." However, if the conflict is part of a broader pattern of bullying or the tactics used to "resolve" it involve bullying, that isn't a normal workplace conflict.

Offering constructive feedback, guidance, or advice about work-related behavior.

The key word here is "constructive." We all should have the emotional intelligence and self-awareness to appreciate our flaws. We are accountable to provide value to our organizations and positively contribute to solving business problems. How are we to improve if no one helps us see our weaknesses, our growth areas, or teaches us how to do something better?

We are a constant "work in progress" and there are always areas for improvement. In a positive work environment, everyone is supported and challenged to learn, grow, and develop. In order to do that, we need to be open and accepting of helpful and reasonable feedback delivered in a respectful way. This takes maturity, humility, and emotional intelligence. Feedback is an essential mechanism for our human evolution.

We own our personal and career development and the self-awareness that we don't know everything. We are responsible for our professional growth. We are accountable for our imperfections and to ensure that we're open to hearing that we have to improve. Organizations need to encourage and even demand that employees continue to develop, improve their performance, and evolve into more talented employees. Adaptability is critical to our personal success (at work and in life).

We need constructive feedback to inspire us to constantly evolve. We may not like what we hear or it may make us uncomfortable, but as long as the delivery mechanism is respectful and fair, this isn't bullying. It's good business practice!

Reasonable actions related to staff performance

Performance management (i.e., managing performance, taking reasonable disciplinary actions, or assigning work) will always be challenging. Communicating that expectations haven't been met isn't easy. Nevertheless, this is still a normal requirement of all organizations and part of sound management. The important word is "reasonable." If you feel sabotaged, gutted, or totally shocked by what you hear, consider whether there is something deeper going on.

Also, if no path for improvement such as training, mentoring, or other mechanism to help you address the performance problem is discussed, or if no performance plan is offered, this is another bad sign. Performance management is about identifying performance issues, supporting staff to collaboratively create a learning plan for improvement, and following through with the plan.

If there is no path for improvement discussed, you might have a boss who needs a lesson in performance management. That is much different than a bully boss. It bears reinforcing that there must be bullying behavior involved in the performance management process for the line to be crossed.

Unpopular, yet defensible decision-related management

Our organizations regularly make strategic decisions and changes that impact our daily work (i.e., resource allocation, solving budget problems, project scale reduction, and scheduling decisions that increase workload). We easily get personally invested in our work. We think we are doing a great job and we believe our projects or our units are the most important. We lose sight of the broader strategic vision or priorities within our organizations.

Our management isn't thinking about the individuals at work – they are accountable for steering the business in alignment with broader mission, vision, and strategic mandates. They often make tough decisions that are focused on strategy to adjust to an ever-changing political, market, environmental, or industry landscape.

Embracing change and agility is a hallmark of most successful organizations. Defensible management decisions that are unpopular (i.e., shutting down a program or project, merging with another business, shifting business models, etc.) are common. When priorities, customer requirements, budgets, or management decisions negatively impact our work, it's easy to lash out when faced with how the decision impacts our work and to express our personal disappointment.

It's perfectly acceptable to disagree with management's approach. We may feel anger, disgust, and betrayal when a decision negatively affects our work. However, I suggest that we try to step back from our emotions and evaluate the grounds for the decision. If we find merit or at least a legitimate reason behind the decision, we may have to learn to live with it.

While the decision may not be appreciated, as long as it's defensible and aligns with broader organizational goals, we have to show maturity, flexibility, and the capacity to adapt. We are accountable for getting back on the bus and not gossiping or sabotaging the people who made the decision. Emotional maturity and resilience are critical. It's understandable and acceptable that we dislike the change but we can't respond by being insubordinate.

Broad management decisions that impact the entire organization or a particular project, program, or unit are normal. However, if the decision is flavored with revenge, manipulation, sabotage, or personal humiliation, the possibility of bullying surfaces. If the decision is easily linked with a pattern of targeted action against a person or a group of staff, take note. Further, if the decision has a particularly negative impact on you individually and it feels like you actually have been singled out for different treatment from your colleagues, a red flag should go up.

***

The key is to approach each situation with a reasonable, objective perspective in order to properly assess if there is bullying involved. Seek the advice from trusted colleagues or human resource specialists (but, it is best not to ask those within your organization for help until you've received credible, unbiased advice). Ask experienced mentors who are outside of your workplace to provide their insight.

There may also be helpful tools within or external to your organization to help you evaluate the situation. For example, as a certified project manager, I have access to the Project Management Institute's ethics tools and the five-step *Ethical Decision-Making Framework*[14] to assist in analyzing tough situations. I also have access to ethics and professional conduct resources through my law society. Perhaps your organization has an Employee Assistance Program that provides confidential professional resources to help you sort out a problem. Perhaps you are part of a professional association that could assist. Use these tools if you can. There's nothing more helpful than sound, sober, objective analysis and advice. We often need help seeing the forest amongst the trees.

What Motivates the Bully?

I find it's usually the bullies who are the most insecure.

- Tom Felton[15]

Likely the second most common (and totally understandable) question is: "Why do bullies bully?" The answer lies in a complex web of jealousy, insecurity, and inadequacy wrapped in a blanket of narcissism and egoism.

Bullies target those who they fear will steal the attention away from them or those who they are envious of (usually because the target is highly regarded and popular – exactly what the bully isn't). In effect, that means if you are highly skilled, experienced, regarded, and ethical, you represent a threat. The bully very purposefully selects the target and begins a campaign of undermining and destruction to ensure the threat is eliminated.

Following a militaristic command methodology, bullies generally approach their targets using fear, intimidation, and threats. Mark, a bullying target, described how afraid he was to speak up and that he felt he was working for a "workplace terrorist." I've already used this point of reference in the book. It seems extreme, but it is one of the most accurate descriptions for bullies I have heard. Bullies are malicious, arrogant, sneaky, and underhanded. They commonly treat people like children. They encourage conflict and above all, they create a work environment rife with stress and fear.

Bullies may also struggle with an element of mental illness that those who have the proper medical training can diagnose. While I have made it clear that I'm not a psychiatrist, psychologist, or social worker, medical practitioners and other trained professionals have documented that bullies often have narcissistic personality disorders or tendencies. They may also have deep-rooted insecurities and have been victims of mental and/or physical abuse. They may have lived in homes where bullying was normal and learned it as a useful survival skill.

I can't comment on how to diagnose whether a bully has a narcissistic personality disorder, sociopathic tendencies, or any other mental health issue. However, I will say that I've spoken with many people impacted by bullies at work and there is, without doubt, a common thread of mental health issues that seems to run through many of our experiences. The most common thread is narcissism and a lack of empathy.

While mental illness can't be used to condone or justify a bully's actions, it is reassuring to know it might be a factor in explaining their dysfunctional personality. The more that we understand the bullies at work, the better we will be at finding ways to deal with them effectively.

It takes a while to grasp that bullies rarely have much, if any, capacity to care or feel compassion for others (and that usually leaks into their personal lives). From the many stories I've been told, it is fair to say that they are usually consumed by their egos. They are driven, at all costs, to prove themselves and disprove those around them to ensure they are in the limelight. They need recognition and are constantly on the promotion track. They are control freaks and don't see any other perspective but their own. They hide their deep-rooted inadequacy in a shield and image of impenetrable power and ruthless wielding of authority. The second something goes wrong, they are pointing the finger at others, blaming them as the root cause of the problem. From "fake news" to outright lies, I've heard countless tactics that bullies have used to deflect issues or problems away from them.

There is a clear message that should anyone dare question or challenge their authority, the punishment will be swift and severe. For example, Kelly worked with a bully who proudly announced that someone whom he thought had made a poor decision had been promptly fired. He said it with a remarkable sense of satisfaction and an underlying tone of power and fear.

Job security is a very common threat used by bullies. Karthik shared that his bully enjoyed announcing at meetings that staff cuts were taking place. She specifically noted that there were people in her unit that needed to "get their act together," making references to projects that he was involved in. This not-so-thinly veiled threat left him constantly fearing that he could lose his job at any time. He went to work each day after another anxiety-filled night worrying that "today my boss will joyfully fire me."

Bullies use their image of being cutthroat, powerful, and mean-spirited to their advantage as a scare tactic for submission. Sharon's bully actually took pleasure when introducing himself to new people, referencing that his reputation had likely preceded him (and he was proud of that).

In Joe's story about the bully in his life, Joe was punished for creating a team that "liked him." The bully actually noted that it was imperative that "subordinates fear you." That choice of words is quintessential bullying behavior.

Bullies also commonly make decisions that cross ethical boundaries and breach organizational policies. Bullies don't believe the rules apply to them and that in order to get the results that drive their ego, any tactic is acceptable. David's organization had very clear policies supporting work/life balance, families, and alternate work arrangements. Nonetheless, his bully manager refused to allow any women to work anything but an inflexible full-time schedule.

When approached with a situation relating to a very short-term arrangement for one of his staff with a family challenge, David's bully boss bragged that the predominantly female team had no one working part-time and that it never would "under his watch." He bluntly refused a reasonable request aligned perfectly with the organizational policies on principal, even noting that the employee's poor choice of family arrangement wasn't his or David's problem. David was left trying to explain to his employee that, despite clear supportive organizational policy, he was unable to help her. The saddest piece of his story is that his employee totally understood and expected this result. She knew that she was indirectly (or in this case directly) one of the bully's targets because she had, in her words "stepped out of line."

Finally, it is almost a given that the bully will have senior management under her charm and in her favor. They are masters of political games and openly engage in self-promotion. Erica Pinsky's book *Road to Respect: Path to Profit* is helpful on this topic. She notes:

> *Typically, bulies are very clever and manipulative. The face they present to their own bosses is charming, solicit, and agreeable. Their managers usually view them as efficient, able to deal with touchy issues and situations, someone who gets results.*[16]

***

Therein lies our challenge. While ruining lives of the targets, bullies are pleasant, sycophantic, and manipulative to the executives, supervisors, and human resource personnel. A direct consequence of those perceived short-term "great results" for which they always take credit are the many people left in the bully's wake, suffering untold physical and mental problems. Also, looking in the long-term, the financial, HR, employee turnover, team dysfunction, and stakeholder impacts resulting from a bully are potentially staggering – all of which will be discussed in other chapters.

The Prevalence of Workplace Bullying

> *Bullying is a national epidemic.*

> —Macklemore[17]

Workplace bullying is everywhere, in every sector, workforce, and country – and the levels of its prevalence should send shivers of concern through any organizational leader. In a February 2015 article in the *Financial Post*, Ray Williams notes:

> *Workplace bullying has become a silent epidemic in North America, one that has huge hidden costs in terms of employee well-being and productivity.*[18]

The percentage of people bullied will vary based on country, industry, gender, organizational culture, and many other factors. I have heard stories from targets around the world. However, rather than relying on anecdotal references, for this section, I have relied on the research and statistics of others.

To begin, according to a 2013 *Harvard Business Review* article, over the last few decades, the number of people who've admitted to being the target of workplace bullying has increased drastically.[19] The Workplace Bullying Institute conducted a 2014 survey on the prevalence of bullying in the workplace in the United States. The overall survey results are very clear (and quite shocking). Out of 1,000 people surveyed, 7 out of 10 workers are affected by workplace bullying. Twenty-seven percent responded that they have been or are currently being bullied.[20]

Other recent research indicates that the prevalence of bullying is even higher. Jennifer Grasz reports that 35% of the workforce is bullied.[21] According to Clare Rayner and Ståle Einarsen, both respected bullying researchers, 53%[22] of the workforce is bullied and even up to 75%[23] of the workforce is bullied. In a 2015 *Computer Weekly* article, a survey of 860 IT workers in the United Kingdom showed that 65% believed they had been bullied at work.[24]

***

The statistics are sobering. Bullies are prevalent and the harm they cause has direct impacts on people, workplace harmony, and profits/success. If there is a bully operating in your midst, the impact on the team will be toxic, which inevitably has negative broader impacts for the organization. However, there are many actions that you can take to effectively respond to a bully, regardless of your role in your organization. I address how to create practical action plans to counteract bullies in Chapter 15.

2

Other Disrespectful Behaviors

*Good manners will open doors that
the best education cannot.*

—Clarence Thomas,
Associate Justice of the U.S Supreme Court[25]

Rudeness/Competitiveness

What do you do if you have a difficult, aggressive boss? How can you manage an intensely competitive and rude colleague? Is it bullying, bad manners, or merely normal competition within a workplace? In order to be able to answer these questions it's important to have the objectivity and tools to contrast normal competitive work behavior with rudeness and bullying.

As a sad starting point, many would argue that bad manners are almost the norm in today's self-oriented, competitive world. Rudeness may be acceptable in some places. So you have to begin by setting the bar at a reasonable and appropriate place. Context is important and your analysis should begin from a starting place that aligns with the workplace culture. If you work at a place that is known for its cutthroat culture, then approach the review from this informed position.

Mohammed worked at a large technology company. He was feeling beaten up and diminished. His boss regularly berated him and his team, using words like "idiots," "losers," and "morons." The team's work was never good enough. The expectations were unreasonable and unattainable. At first, Mohammed concluded that his boss was a bully. However, upon objective reflection, he realized all managers in the company seemed to have this leadership style. It was a "survival of the fittest" workplace culture; Mohammed concluded that he was working in a Darwinian organization. The culture wasn't going to change. His boss was rude and demeaning, but he treated everyone like that. In fact, this was the status quo for all managers in the organization.

These situations require introspection. It's very easy to say, "My boss, Allen, is a jerk." Allen may actually be a jerk – but perhaps you work in a highly competitive culture or one that doesn't prioritize politeness. That is what Mohammed discovered. In other words, observe the workplace culture in order to establish what is the norm.

Healthy competition and even some assertive challenge can make for a creative work environment where people push one another to better performance. This is very typical in high tech and other innovation-focused workplaces. However, some organizations turn competition into a fear- and ridicule-based culture.

Once you have gained an objective appreciation for the workplace culture, you can analyze whether you are facing a bully or just an ill-mannered colleague. As a first step, when trying to discern the ethos of your workplace conflict, it is helpful to ask yourself whether you're being overly sensitive or misinterpreting the situation. Step back and look at the situation; try to separate emotion from the behavior. Personal accountability is an effective filter and the situation is rarely one-sided. Self-evaluation can be tough. I suggest that you get a second opinion from someone you trust—someone who will tell you the truth, not just what you want to hear.

Upon completion of this assessment, it is common that you've experienced bad manners and/or poor communication as a starting point. It is also possible that you may have contributed to the dysfunction. Regardless, the least effective means to resolve conflict is sitting back and doing nothing. The situation won't resolve itself. The only way that your relationship will improve is by talking about it and respectfully engaging in a process to reason things out.

The next step is to formulate an appropriate engagement strategy. As a firm believer in self-improvement, I recommend that you hold yourself accountable for your contributions. A lot of positive results in conflict resolution begin after a sincere apology has been made. The next, and often difficult, step is to attempt to directly engage with the offender and explain that you don't appreciate being treated rudely.

Hopefully, she will also be accountable for her poor behavior and you can both move on with some new boundaries for behavior in place. If there are no amends made or behavior alterations, you may need to consider getting your manager or other influencers involved.

However, if you feel the behavior is more than rudeness, I recommend that you review the definition of bullying in order to evaluate whether you've got a much bigger problem on your hands. There is an objective and, in my opinion, clear line between rudeness and bullying. As already noted, the most important evaluation criteria are whether the behavior is repetitive, disrespectful, deliberate, and always for the bully's benefit. If you determine you are dealing with a bully, there is other advice and action plans provided in later chapters to assist.

Harassment

Harassment means different things in different jurisdictions. It may have a more serious legal connotation or it may be what is commonly referred to as "unacceptable workplace behavior" as laid out in your organization's Respectful Workplace Policy. It is, therefore, important to understand the general meaning of the word "harassment" in your workplace and jurisdiction when comparing bullying to harassment.

As a lawyer, I prefer to not use the word "harassment" to describe disrespectful workplace behavior. For those of us in the legal profession, harassment historically connotes sexual misconduct within the context of a hostile work environment. Harassment has more narrow points of reference. It also has potentially criminal consequences that send legal alarm bells off. If you are the victim of sexual misconduct, my advice is to seek the assistance of the police and, if you feel it is needed, obtain legal advice. You must take action to ensure your personal safety as the first priority. This is a serious matter that requires specially trained professionals and experts.

Regardless of my personal bias against the use of the word harassment, in some Western countries and organizations, "harassment" is synonymous with "unacceptable workplace behavior" as defined in many workplace respect policies. In such places, "harassment" has even replaced "unacceptable workplace behavior." For example, in Canada, the federal government's respectful workplace policy is actually called the Policy on Harassment Prevention and Resolution. Harassment is defined as:

> *Improper conduct by an individual, that is directed at and offensive to another individual in the workplace, including at any event or any location related to work, and that the individual knew or ought reasonably to have known would cause offence or harm. It comprises objectionable act(s), comment(s), or display(s) that demean,*

belittle, or cause personal humiliation or embarrassment, and any act of intimidation or threat.[26]

This definition is very similar to the definition of "unacceptable workplace behavior" that is used in most respectful workplace policies, as you'll see in Chapter 9.

Provided you are dealing with a definition of "harassment" that is associated with a Respectful Workplace Policy, the same conclusions can be drawn. Bullying takes place in a disrespectful workplace and may look and feel like harassment within most of these policies. In this context, bullying is a clear violation of the policy against harassment with the same internal processes and challenges already discussed.

If, however, you live and work in a jurisdiction where harassment is a reference to potentially criminal behavior, and you feel that you are facing such a situation, seeking the advice of policing and legal professionals is best advised. See also the section on Discriminatory Workplace Harassment in Chapter 7 for guidance.

Workplace Violence

Fortunately, it is very rare for a bully to resort to violence. While bullying is clearly the equivalent of psychological assault, it is highly unusual to result in or involve physical assault of the target. Bullies prefer to break a target's spirit rather than his bones.

One point that bears noting is the possibility that targets of bullying who have reached the end of their tolerance and capacity to think clearly may be more likely to act out. In an article in LiveScience.com, the stress that a target feels is described as follows:

> *This is why a person can't make quality decisions... They can't even consider alternatives.*

Just like a battered spouse, they don't even perceive alternatives to their situations when they're stressed and depressed and under attack.[27]

When a target has been beaten down to the point of considering suicide, it is understandable that they might consider revenge or retribution against the bully or the leaders of the organization who the target thinks supported the bully. However, even in extreme cases, rather than respond with violence towards the bully, the victim is more likely to turn the violence inward, resulting in documented cases of target suicide.

***

Distinguishing bullying from rudeness, harassment, and workplace violence requires analysis. Review the definition of bullying and common behaviors. Consider your workplace culture. Assess your contributions to the situation, if any. These steps usually provide the clarity needed to decide what kind of behavior you are facing.

3

Bullying Isn't a "Leadership Style"

Outstanding leaders go out of their way to boost the self-esteem of their personnel. If people believe in themselves, it's amazing what they can accomplish.

—Sam Walton,
Co-Founder of Wal-Mart[28]

There is nothing that I find more distasteful than organizational attempts to diminish a bully's acts by describing them as a "leadership style." First and foremost, bullying is the *opposite* of leadership. Any reference to the contrary is simply untrue. Behavior that creates an intimidating, chaotic, dysfunctional, or humiliating work environment can't possibly be leadership. Second, such inaccurate references indirectly support and condone the behavior. Third, those who are legitimate leaders have their skills marginalized when an executive equates true leadership to bullying.

For the sake of education, it's worth conducting an item-by-item comparison of the characteristics of leaders and bullies.

Leaders	Bullies
Encourage	Demotivate/dictate
Set good example	Disrupt/aggressive
Show integrity	Lack integrity
Demonstrate accountability	Avoid responsibility
Build	Destroy
Resolve conflict	Create conflict
Fair/mature	Unfair/immature

Leaders inspire and build functional teams. They value others, reward competence, and encourage contribution. They set good examples, holding themselves to the same high standards they expect of others. They aim for clarity. Behaving with maturity, they take responsibility for their mistakes. They let others work without interference. They resolve conflicts in fair, supportive ways.

By contrast, bullies erode and disrupt functional teams. They may use team language but they're not team players. They devalue others. They are threatened by the competence of others. They stifle contribution. They set bad examples and exhibit hypocrisy. They pollute the workplace by projecting their own negativity onto others, creating confusion and uncertainty. They lack integrity and maturity. They lie and blame others to disguise their own failings. They focus on petty fault finding. They generate conflict.

If you hear an executive describing a bully as a leader, my best advice is to take note and appreciate that the workplace culture likely tolerates or supports bullying. Be careful about expressing your opposing opinion about the bully. It may make your situation worse. If you work in an organization run by a bully, know that the likelihood of a chaos-filled and toxic workplace is almost a certainty.

The truth may be sobering but with knowledge comes

the power to choose (if you can) to successfully initiate and implement an exit strategy to a more respectful and harmonious work environment. In some situations, the best strategy will be an action plan that works towards an exit strategy. Accepting reality will lead you to a path of self-preservation.

For example, I failed to appreciate how entrenched and protected the bully that I worked for was. I was also unrealistic when I chose an action plan to report the bully and expected positive change. I was naïve and placed faith in policies and processes that weren't enforced. In hindsight, I wished I had been able to see the only thing that would change the situation was if I left my dysfunctional, toxic workplace.

All of which is to say, I hope that you will avoid my mistakes and take more time to assess the power dynamics when you craft your plan for dealing with your bully.

***

Don't let anyone try to tell you differently – bullying is the antithesis of leadership. Nor is it a style of managing. It is a recipe for mayhem, organizational dysfunction, turmoil, and failure. I've said this already but again reinforce that it is the equivalent of workplace terrorism.

4
Who Are the Most Common Targets?

The purpose of human life is to serve, and to show compassion and the will to help others.
—Albert Schweitzer[29]

Unlike schoolyard bullying, people in the workplace are not targeted because they are perceived as loners, outcasts, different, or weak. Most likely, they are targeted because of their abilities, likeability, or other positive characteristics that may have posed a threat to the bully. The perception of threat is entirely in his mind, but it's what he feels and believes.

I believe that the most innovative, hardworking, and talented employees are often perceived as threats because they are drawing attention, accolades, and people toward their work – likely away from the bully or his projects.

Jonathan was one of the most respected and experienced employees in his unit. Until his boss was transferred into his unit, he also was a top performer, always ready to go beyond. He enjoyed complex projects, challenging himself to learn. He had received awards and accolades from every supervisor he had ever worked with. Then Anne-Marie arrived. She quickly realized Jonathan was very bright, revered, and a star performer. She found this intimidating and instantly began her bullying campaign of interpersonal destruction against Jonathan, ruining his career and confidence.

The Workplace Bullying Institute's research findings from a 2000 study[30] confirm that targets are usually veterans and the most highly skilled persons in the workgroup. Common attributes of targets often include the following:

- Targets are independent.
- Targets are more technically skilled than their bullies.
- They are the "go-to" veteran workers to whom new employees turn for guidance.
- Targets are better liked.
- They have more social skills and, quite likely, possess greater emotional intelligence.
- Colleagues, customers, and management appreciate the warmth that the targets bring to the workplace.
- Targets are ethical and honest.
- Targets are people with personalities founded on a nurturing and social orientation – a desire to help, heal, teach, develop, and nurture others.

***

The logic for eliminating a team member with such enviable skills and talent makes no sense unless you focus on the "enviable." Instead of rewarding the target for her exceptional contributions and assistance in helping the bully achieve results, targets are singled out for abuse and mistreatment. Bullies intentionally identify and take calculated steps to kill the target's reputation, spirit, and self-esteem, driving them from workplace. It bears reminding that bullies are seeking all the attention – anything that takes the spotlight away from them must be removed. Remember – they play a zero-sum game.

5

What Are the Most Common Bullying Scenarios?

Not everyone has been a bully or the victim of bullies, but everyone has seen bullying, and seeing it, has responded to it by joining in or objecting, by laughing or keeping silent, by feeling disgusted or feeling interested.

—Octavia E. Butler[31]

Generally speaking, bullies most often target those underneath in the organizational hierarchy. This translates into a simple fact – the majority of bullies are bosses. According to the Workplace Bullying Institute 56% of bullies choose a subordinate as their target.[32] This is why the situation is so difficult for the target. If they complain, the natural and often effective response from the bully is that the target is a poor performer and using the complaint as a tactic to deflect attention away from this problem.

Being adept at deceit, bullies paint a very negative picture of the target that HR usually supports. HR then circles the wagons in defense when one of their own is accused. This makes the odds of a fair and successful target complaint less than ideal.

Even more distressing is that in private and, if they feel they can be honest, human resource personnel invariably will admit that the boss is a bully (or at least they wouldn't want to work for him). Often, they also feel like they have been "told" what to do by the bully and feel intimidated. The bully usually has friends in high places and HR feels pressure to fall in line.

Susan shared her bullying story beginning with a startling comment – "We just fired the second bully vice president in two years." While she wasn't the target, she worked in a role that allowed her to observe from a distance. Her experience with HR was what concerned her the most. Not only did they protect the bullies at first, they created plans to deal with the targets instead of the bullies. They believed the targets were a bigger risk to the company than the bullies. Fearing lawsuits, sabotage, sick leave claims, and public relations problems, HR empowered the bullies.

Susan had the chance to discuss the situation with a senior HR member after the second bully was fired. Her colleague not only admitted that she was fully aware that both the vice presidents were bullies, but also that she feared she would become a target if she didn't support them.

Susan was astonished – when replacing the first bully with his mentor, the company failed to consider the obvious. Bully Eduardo was replaced by Bully Jessica who learned all she needed to know about how to succeed as a bully from Eduardo. While the company eventually solved the real problem, it took them two vice presidents and enormous resources to eliminate the bullies and reset the workplace culture.

Bullies take on colleagues about one third of the time. The bully perceives a coworker as competition, perhaps for a promotion. It's the same game, just with a different person in the crosshairs.

Very rarely does a workplace bully "bully up," taking on someone of higher rank. Instead, they apply their manipulative social skill, ensuring those above protect them.

Commonly called "obsequious," "brown-nosers," "ass kissers," bullies are pros at playing the game of Suck Up. They simply focus on "getting those outstanding results" and "taking care of the problems no one else seems to be able to solve." By ingratiating themselves, bullies ensure they are virtually untouchable (at least that is how they view it).

***

Most of the time, the bully is your boss or supervisor. This dynamic creates a challenging environment for targets, both for coping with and for complaining about the bully. However, there are many practical tools that you have in your "Bully Be Gone" toolkit to help you cope. We will discuss ways to manage and even confront the problem in Chapter 15, with action plans for everyone impacted by bullying.

6

The Impacts of Workplace Bullying

*The great aim of education is
not knowledge but action.*
—Herbert Spencer[33]

As previously noted, the impacts of bullying are widespread and significant. In order to make sense of the depth and breadth of the types of impact, the diagram on page 44 is helpful. I view bullying through a pyramidal lens with the targets forming the foundation and the layers of other people and types of impacts rising above. The pyramid is designed with a purpose.

Many business leaders would likely say that bullying is wrong, but not all recognize that it has tangible and significant organizational costs or where those costs and impacts are felt. I firmly believe that the key to eradicating workplace bullying is with education and all of us taking action against it. Once organizations solidly appreciate how one bully's actions can permeate throughout the workplace, causing extraordinary impacts, and their staff are standing up against it, workplace bullying will cease.

In order to respond to a skeptical executive, politician, or senior manager, it helps to have clear information about each cost/impact. Use the information to tailor-make an approach to focus on the areas about which the influencer is most concerned. By putting ourselves in the world of the leaders, modeling the conversation on identifying topics or statistics that resonate in their world, I believe we can influence change. Hopefully, we can keep them up at night until they take real action.

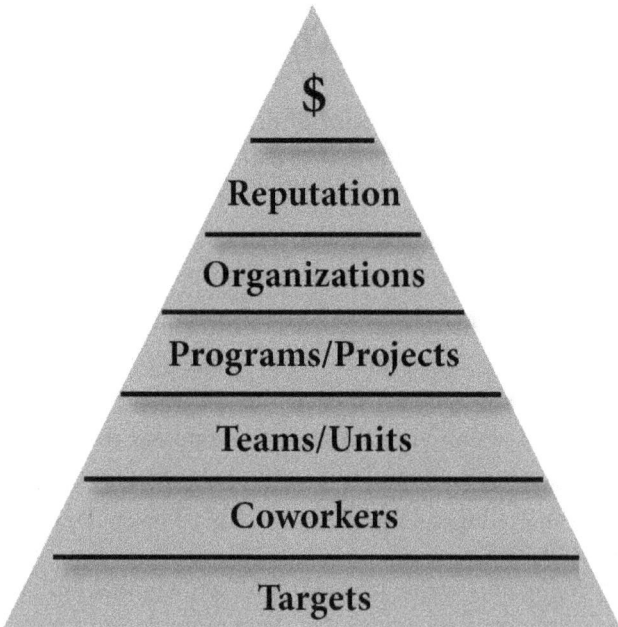

The pyramid shows the escalation of impacts on organizations and drives the lesson in awareness. As each layer is revealed, objective and persuasive evidence mounts. Cost/impacts caused by bullies can be categorized and analyzed into a series of buckets, each having potentially more significant impact.

Regardless of where we fit in the organizational hierarchy, as sad as it may seem, I believe we need to see "what's in it for me" in order to be motivated to change. Once everyone is on the same page, armed with their own reasons for embracing an anti-bullying agenda, only then will organizational behavior change. It clearly helps if leaders set the example – but there also needs to be individual accountability and motivation. I hope the pyramid provides information that acts as a motivational catalyst for change for everyone. Particularly as we reach the top levels of the structure, I believe that leaders will fully comprehend that bullies are simply bad for business, regardless of what business they are in.

The following is an analysis of each one of the pyramidal layers.

a) **Targets**

Targets of bullying face terrible impacts. Narrowing our impact discussion to the lives of targets is a sobering reality check. There are many researched and documented negative health impacts that can be attributed to bullying. One of the leading authors on the dire consequences of the impact of workplace bullying is professor Ståle Einarsen. He has completed a significant body of research and articles on this topic, all of which supports my conclusions.[34]

These well-documented negative impacts often slowly creep up, likely due to prolonged stress experienced by targets that deteriorate their physical or mental health.

Unfortunately, most targeted people try to "tough it out." This rarely stops the bullying and it allows the overwhelming stress to build. The stress will not end until the bullying ceases or the target is separated from the source of the stressors – the bully and the organization condoning her.

Bullying affects both the brain and body. I have broken the discussion of the health impacts of bullying into two categories: physical injuries and psychological injuries.

Physical Injuries

Stress-related diseases and health complications from prolonged exposure to the stressors of bullying that have been reported include, but are not limited to:

- Cardiovascular impacts: heart attacks, hypertension, strokes
- Gastrointestinal problems: irritable bowel syndrome, colitis
- Infections
- Auto-immune disorders: fibromyalgia, chronic fatigue syndrome
- Diabetes
- Skin disorders

Psychological-Emotional-Mental Injuries

There is no better description of the mental impact of bullying than the following:

> Bullying is often called psychological harassment or violence. What makes it psychological is its impact on the person's mental health and sense of well-being. The personalized, focused nature of the assault destabilizes and disassembles the target's identity, ego, strength, and ability to rebound from the assaults. The longer the exposure to stressors like bullying, the more severe the psychological impact upon the Target.[35]

Psychological injuries caused by bullying include[36]:

- Debilitating anxiety
- Panic attacks
- Clinical depression
- Post-traumatic stress (PTSD)
- Suicide

Targets of bullying also routinely respond to the

abuse, usually in a fashion that harms the organization rather than the bully. These impacts can have unexpected consequences for the employer. For example, through a poll conducted by the Workplace Bullying Institute[37] of 800 managers and employees in 17 industries, targets reported as follows:

> *Among workers who've been on the receiving end of bullying:*
> - *48% intentionally decreased their work effort*
> - *47% intentionally decreased the time spent at work*
> - *38% intentionally decreased the quality of their work*
> - *63% lost work time avoiding the offender*
> - *66% said their performance declined*
> - *12% said they left their job*

These results align with the many stories that targets have shared with me and with my personal experience. As the bully's attack intensifies, the target's commitment to their work diminishes. They often punish their offenders and the organization. This information alone should send a chill up any senior manager's spine. Anything that can harm productivity and program success is worth looking at more closely.

b) Coworkers/Colleagues

Coworkers often suffer some of the same physical and mental impacts that targets do as a result of their direct engagement with both the bully and the target. They are caught in the web of chaos and find work a place of conflict, distress, and discomfort.

Coworkers also struggle emotionally, experiencing stress observing the bully. They also worry about the impacts on both themselves and their colleagues. They spend energy, caught in the middle and torn between supporting the target and protecting themselves from the bully. They take more stress and sick days than happy employees. They regularly look for work in a more harmonious organization.

Luis told me that he felt powerless, guilty, and afraid every day at work. He watched his coworker being bullied and was immobilized by fear of becoming the target. He did nothing. He felt awful. He found another job, but two years after leaving he still was carrying around the burden of "failing to take action."

c) Teams/Units

Bullying creates a toxic and stressful work environment for all those who work with the bully, regardless of who is the target. Productivity, performance, creativity, and team spirit deteriorate. Bullies prevent work from getting done, causing confusion and a loss of focus. Most executives will give their ear if you ask to talk about an issue related to productivity.

In a 2014 *Guardian Newspaper* article on the problems created by workplace bullying, writer Ian Erickson discussed how workplace bullying harms teams.[38] He noted that:

> Bullying...is behaviour that prevents work from being finished. Losses are caused by staff members struggling to cope at work, high rates of absenteeism and talented employees leaving in favour of a more harmonious place of employment.

Experiments and other reports offer additional insights about the effects of bullying. Not unexpectedly, they highlight that team and individual creativity suffer, team performance decreases and team spirit fades.

There is also a lost opportunity cost that can be quantified. That means that when the more talented target is driven from work, either through termination, constructive discharge, or quitting, the company loses the value that worker created. Further, the demotivated and stressed-out team that is left behind rarely recovers. Synergy, team commitment, and high performance are vital to success. Once that has been lost, particularly in a traumatic bullying drama, most teams fail to re-engage.

d) Programs/Projects

Virtually every organizational output is produced through a structured program or project. Having had the honor of many speaking presentations to global project, program, and portfolio professionals on the topic of bullying in project management, I've heard firsthand the stories of many failures, delays, and costs associated with bullies. Projects are subsets of workplaces and since project and program management is, for the most part, an activity that involves working very closely with others, the impact of a bully in a program or project is potentially lethal to success.

The workplace culture in many projects is pressure-filled and challenged by time, budget, and scope restraints. Many projects are competing for attention, priority, and resources. This is a perfect environment for a bully to use tactics to eliminate the perceived competition and take all the glory for any project successes.

Since the target is usually a "go-to veteran," the bully creates a talent vacuum where the best workers effectively cease engagement. You can imagine how that impacts the completion of the work itself. Unfortunately, bullies have a myopic view of the world and are unable to see they are effectively self-sabotaging.

Further, program/project managers infrequently have enough positional authority to carry out their responsibilities. Most projects also occur in organizations where project team members report, not only to the project manager but to a line manager as well. Consequently, they must increasingly rely on other indirect methods to motivate team members to accomplish the needed project work. The most effective of these other methods is by forming relationships with team members and influencers. Once again, that is precisely the kind of situation bullies can exploit.

In summary, bullies have deep and direct negative impacts on programs and projects. The division, demotivation, and confusion they create reduce innovation, engagement, and productivity. Finally, with the most experienced team motivators sidelined many projects suffer financially and delays are commonplace. Simply put – bullies prevent work from getting done.

e) Organizations

As the "single most preventable and needless expense on a company's register" bullying is harmful to business productivity and workplace harmony. If commitments aren't fulfilled on time, budget, or scope, the impact ripples throughout the organization. Bluntly put, ending bullying is just plain good for business.

We've already touched upon how bullying impacts performance and productivity with self-evident results. We've also touched upon how bullies create a conflict-filled and disagreeable workplace culture. Without workplace harmony, further impacts occur that are most often seen by the human resources team.

There is also a direct link between bullying and sick-leave/disability claims. The stress and health impacts caused by bullying affects not only profits when top talent takes time off work, but also requires the engagement of HR personnel to manage each situation. Bullied people (and their coworkers) often end up quitting for one reason or another. This has a significant negative impact on success, especially when the organization has to replace the best and brightest (the bullied ones and their coworkers).

Employee turnover costs are incurred and include employer contributions to retirement plans for the departed worker, head hunter/recruiting firm fees, time spent by managers and HR staff, hiring bonuses/incentives, and the harder-to-calculate lost production during the entire process that must be made up by coworkers.

The first place HR often turns to for advice is legal professionals. Time spent risk managing, strategizing, and preparing to respond with lawyers involved add up quickly. It is becoming more common for targets to turn to legal recourse to solve the problem, costing enormous amounts of time, stress, and money.

Further, courts are becoming more aware of workplace bullying with expected negative results for the companies that are found to have condoned the bully. Finally, severance costs regularly factor in. All tolled, a single bully can cause hundreds of thousands and even millions of dollars in costs if just one well-founded claim is successful, even before the matter gets anywhere near a court.

It is incredible what one bully can do to even a multi-billion dollar enterprise. If you need just one recent and highly publicized example to highlight this point, Google "Harvey Weinstein." Carl shared his story of the estimated costs that a bullying manager caused his company. Focusing exclusively on quantifying the impacts, he estimated that the direct loss was over a million dollars. Adding up the cost of the bullying investigation, experts, legal fees, severance costs, talent departure, sick leave, and HR time, the organization was left holding a seven-figure bill. To add salt to the wound, the bully they protected left the company within weeks of the "resolution" of the matter.

f) **Reputation**

Under the heading of reputation, there are two very different impacts to consider. The first, and most obvious, is the potential impact on the organization's reputation in the eyes of the world and their stakeholders. Recently, the world witnessed Volkswagen's 2015 meteoric fall from grace losing billions of euros in share value and potentially jeopardizing the corporation's future. All thanks to a decision somewhere within the organization to choose to falsely improve emission results using a deviant piece of technology.

The world instantly and fittingly responded. Shame was heaped on the company because they chose profits over ethics. This is a terrific lesson and wake-up call for all organizations and plays perfectly into the issue of workplace bullying. Reputations that have taken years to establish can be ruined in one article about a bully executive, one bullying investigation, one person starting a legal action against the organization that protected a bully.

The 2015 media frenzy about the alleged Darwinian work environment at Amazon proves that bullying can have serious impacts on organizational reputation. If your workplace is perceived as toxic, people inevitably gossip about it. They share their frustration with anyone willing to listen, which, in the case of Amazon, led to journalist engagement from the *New York Times*.[39] Think of what such an event costs in public relations, communications, and lost time – a reputational event of Titanic proportions.

People are less likely to do business with a company harboring a bully, even if the bullying isn't directed at them. All they have to see or even hear about is the bully treating staff poorly. Disrespectful behavior makes people uncomfortable. People will judge organizations harshly. The tide is definitely turning towards a marketplace that is aware of the impacts of workplace bullying and won't support organizations that don't get on board.

The second aspect of reputation relates to the personal reputation of the executives that condone a bullying workplace culture. Almost every executive is (or should be) concerned about their own reputation as leaders, success-drivers, and model citizens. Leaders are judged by their actions and their values. Organizational leaders may find their own integrity at risk by protecting or failing to address bullying. Respect, trust, and loyalty are earned – a bully can ruin years of work building these values.

While it is acknowledged that some well-known leaders seem impervious to this concern, if you look a little closer, you may find they are bullies themselves. Are they actual devils wearing Prada? There are very few organizational leaders that would be insulated from the possibility of termination if faced with a Volkswagen "cheat device" event. Leaders beware – your reputation and job security could be at stake if you fail to address your workplace bullies.

g) Profits and Share Value

At the top of the pyramid in terms of issues that every senior executive worries about are profit and share value. There are direct negative and financial impacts that bullying has on the bottom line. Our challenge is pushing organizations to revise their focus on short-term results (which bullies are experts at achieving) to take a longer-term approach.

Getting the attention of senior management is never easy but one thing helps – cold, clear facts that objectify the problem and highlight the opportunity cost of not resolving it. In order to convince the skeptics, it may help to have some reliable data to shore up the argument that bullying is bad for business.

As already noted, in his 2014 *Guardian* article on the problems created by workplace bullying, writer Ian Erickson, references an article in which New Zealander Shane Cowishlaw writes that workplace bullying costs his country hundreds of millions of dollars.[40] Australia reports losses in the billions. Not surprisingly for organizations in the much larger United States, workplace bullying-related costs are estimated to be over $200 billion.

It bears noting the potential impact that a bullying workplace environment can have on share price. Again, using Amazon as a wonderful illustration of market forces at work, Amazon's share price dropped from $535.22 a share on August 17, 2015 to $463.37 one week later. If that doesn't get executives sweating, then I don't know what might.

***

The impacts of bullying are widespread and significant. Viewing bullying through a pyramidal lens with the targets forming the foundation and the layers of other people and types of impacts rising above helps make sense of it all. If organizations begin to recognize how bullies' actions ripple throughout the workplace, I believe bullying will be recognized as simply bad for business. Anything bad for business is therefore likely to be stopped.

7

Is Workplace Bullying Illegal?

I find hope in the darkest of days, and focus in the
brightest. I do not judge the universe.

—Dalai Lama[41]

"Is workplace bullying illegal?" This is a question that I am
often asked and, like many legal questions, the best answer is:
"It depends." It depends mostly on where you live and whether there is human rights or anti-workplace bullying legislation in place. Thus, everyone must ensure that they consult
with legal experts in their jurisdiction in order to determine
whether bullying is illegal.

There is also potentially more than one way in which
bullying could be illegal. I've separated this chapter into sections discussing the potential means by which bullying could
be illegal where you work.

Workplace Bullying Laws

There is a clear legislative trend to make workplace bullying illegal (usually as a health and workplace safety issue).
However, this is very much still evolving in many parts of the
world. At the moment, the world leaders on the anti-bullying

law front are the European Union (with France in the lead), Australia, the United Kingdom, Canada, and New Zealand. All of the countries represented have passed anti-workplace bullying legislation (or the states/provinces that have the legal authority in this domain have done so).

The United States has no national anti-workplace bullying legislation, although one is being proposed and slowly moving through the political processes. As of the date of publication, thirty states and two territories have introduced the Healthy Workplace Bill into their legislatures which, when it becomes law, will radically change the face of workplace bullying in the United States. There is some very interesting media coverage in the U.S. about the anti-bullying bills that have been introduced thus far. For those interested, YouTube has some helpful video materials.

If you are fortunate and live in a jurisdiction that has passed laws making workplace bullying illegal, then you have the luxury of a second layer of protection that is external to the policies of your organization. Generally speaking, once such legislation is passed, organizations are forced to take certain prescribed action to prevent and address workplace bullying. For example, they are often required to implement stronger workplace respect policies that include "bullying" as a prohibited behavior. Commonly, organizations are also required to implement new training initiatives, and procedures for handling bullying complaints, investigations, and resolution.

While they are cumbersome and bureaucratic, even the possibility of an external investigation, publicity, and legal violation is a major motivator for organizations to address workplace bullying in a meaningful way. I am blessed to live in a progressive country and province with anti-workplace bullying legislation that has been in place for almost five years at the date of publication. I've had personal experience with how the legislation works and is enforced. I've also been part of an investigation led by the legal authorities responsible for enforcing the law.

In my situation, the formal workplace bullying complaint I filed while on bully-related sick leave required that my organization report the matter to the authorities. Upon receipt of the complaint, the legal authorities commenced a formal external investigation separate from the internal review that the workplace respect policy required. It was a politically charged matter given its profile, who was accused of being a bully (a senior executive), and the potential negative organizational, reputational, and financial impact.

Both the internal and external investigations were very costly (external consultants, lawyers, HR personnel were involved), time consuming, disruptive and, ultimately, a serious wake-up call for my former workplace. I can only imagine how much time, money, and resources were spent. I knew I could never return to my toxic work environment, so with the help of an employment lawyer, a settlement agreement was negotiated. I never returned to work for that organization.

Subsequent to the investigation, I was told by others who still worked there that the organization established a new annual mandatory anti-workplace bullying training module for all employees. In effect, the investigative experience appears to have motivated them to implement an enhanced anti-bullying awareness policy and campaign and fall into closer alignment with the law.

I'm very grateful for the protection that my province's anti-workplace bullying law provided. It was a powerful tool that forced change upon my former workplace. However, it's important to acknowledge that bullying doesn't disappear overnight once legislation is passed. Nor does a long-standing workplace culture that has supported and promoted bullies.

I worked in a company that continued to support well-known bullies long after the law took effect. They ensured the organization was compliant with the new statutory changes forced on them. However, this was compliance in practice but not in spirit. There was no improvement in the toxic and fear-driven workplace culture after the legislation was passed. The command and control leadership style of the executives remained the same. For years afterward, and until there was a high-profile complaint, the leadership continued to support and promote well-known disrespectful employees and bullies.

For transformational change to take place, organizations and their leaders have to make a conscious decision to change. While the law may motivate such change, it is really a stick as opposed to a carrot if an organization doesn't comply.

If, on the other hand, you work in a jurisdiction where no workplace bullying legislation exists, then you are unfortunately left with internal processes as your only "official" recourse. Sadly, billions of workers in the world fall into this category. Even more depressing is the fact that many organizations in the developing world have yet to establish even the most basic workplace respect policies.

Thus, collectively we have a lot of work to do and it will take time to disrupt the status quo in many places. That being said, the expansion in the number of countries embracing laws against workplace bullying proves that while the movement towards change may be slow, it's already well underway.

Discrimination Laws

Most countries have state/province and federal civil rights laws that are designed to protect workers from discriminatory and disparate mistreatment, commonly referred to in legal terms as "discriminatory workplace harassment." Discriminatory workplace harassment enters the domain of human rights law and becomes quite technical.

If, and only if, you are a member of a protected-status group and you have been mistreated by a person at work (the bully) who is not a member of a protected group might you be able to claim that you were a victim of discriminatory workplace harassment. This confusing statement requires an explanation absent legal jargon.

Discriminatory workplace harassment has a legal foundation that is different from workplace bullying. This foundation is much narrower than behaviors captu

red by a workplace respect policy. While many employers have policies that prohibit bullying-type behavior, these are separate from the issue of discrimination. Erica Pinsky, in her book titled *Road to Respect: Path to Profit,* notes:

> *[Discriminatory] Workplace harassment flows from human rights law...and is very specifically defined...Human rights law was structured in response to historical discrimination in our society.*[42]

In order for an individual to be deemed to be illegally harassing another at work, the victim must be able to prove that they were targeted for their race, gender, age, religion, ethnicity, marital status, sexual orientation, or another ground noted in the law. Only then can the behavior be potentially categorized as a form of illegal discrimination that can be defined as:

> *A type of discrimination and means engaging in a course of annoying comments or conduct that is known or ought reasonably to be known to be unwelcome, that is tied to a prohibited ground of discrimination and that detrimentally affects the work environment or leads to adverse job-related consequences for the victim of harassment.*[43]

In order for the possibility of discriminatory workplace harassment to be involved, there must first be human rights legislation in effect. Second, the bully must be engaging in conduct that is directed to a person in a way that violates what is best described as a prohibited ground of discrimination as provided by the law (i.e. religion, color, sexual orientation, etc.).

Generally, most bullying is "status-blind" harassment. In other words, the bully isn't targeting the victim because she is Asian, Christian, pregnant, gay, or some other identifying trait that is protected by law from discrimination. However, is it estimated that in about 20% of the cases, there is sometimes a link between bullying and discrimination.

For example, let's assume you live in England. The United Kingdom has enacted human rights legislation that declares it illegal to discriminate against anyone on the basis of religion. If a workplace bully targets a person because he is a Muslim and there is proof that his religion was the basis for bullying, then there is the possibility that the bullying is illegal discrimination. If this line has been crossed, there is a chance that the bully could be criminally charged with discriminatory workplace harassment.

The main difference between discriminatory workplace harassment and "normal" workplace bullying is that this is a matter for the legal professionals and authorities to handle. Also, the potential outcomes are a lot more significant. Unlike violations of workplace respect policies, allegations of discrimination are external to an organization involving outside authorities and potentially serious consequences for the bully if proven and convicted.

In addition, this severe type of bullying would also undoubtedly represent a breach of an organization's workplace respect policy. Thus, it is possible that a bully could be both externally and internally investigated and punished for her actions.

***

Workplace bullying can be illegal. However, much depends on interpretations of the laws in place where you live and work (assuming they exist). Seek help from experts if you believe the bullying violates the applicable legislation in your country, state, or province.

8

Employer Responsibility

If you are neutral in situations of injustice, you have chosen the side of the oppressor. If an elephant has its foot on the tail of a mouse, and you say that you are neutral, the mouse will not appreciate your neutrality.

—Desmond Tutu,
South Africa[44]

I believe that employers have both a moral and ethical responsibility to take action. If they remain neutral, bullying will continue. If employers refuse to tolerate bullying in the workplace, it will stop – simple as that.

Regardless of what governments do, the real power to eliminate workplace bullying lies in the hands of employers. In simple terms, employers control and define all work conditions and policies of the workplace. They choose the strategies, values, and workplace behavior expectations. It bears reinforcing that our organizations craft and are accountable for enforcing their own policies on employee conduct, ethics and workplace respect. In fact, organizations delegate the authority to police and enforce these policies to their senior management and human resources. So, bullying – the system – can only be sustained or eliminated by employers.

While it is true that the ultimate responsibility for ethical decision-making and policy enforcement rests with the board of directors, CEO, President, Minister, Managing Director (or their delegates), we all share in this responsibility. We also can't use a lack of authority to shirk this responsibility. It is up to each and every one of us to disrupt the status quo that favors bullies. We must start the movement for change.

Everyone within an organization can play an anti-bullying advocate role to encourage change. Furthermore, the public as consumers and concerned citizens can also take action by voting with their wallets and ballots. The power of shareholders and voters should never be under-estimated. Over time, I believe there will be fewer Amazon stories, fewer organizations ruled by bullies, and more stories about exemplary employers.

Stopping bullying requires nothing less than turning the workplace culture upside down. Bullies must experience negative consequences for harming others. Punishment must replace promotions. Only executives and senior management can reverse the historical trend. To stop bullying requires employers to change the routine ways of "doing business" that have propped up bullies for years.

***

The ultimate responsibility for both the cause and cure for bullying rest squarely on the shoulders of senior management and executives. They put people in harm's way and they can provide safety by undoing the culture that allowed bullying to flourish. However, we all can assist in ensuring our organizations enforce their own policies. We share an ethical responsibility to "blow the whistle," do the right thing. We have an individual duty to be advocates of professionalism, integrity, social justice and ethics.

9

Organizational Approaches to Workplace Bullying

Willingness to change is a strength, even if it means plunging part of the company into total confusion for a while.

—Jack Welch[45]

Many of us don't know where to begin when we are faced with a bullying situation. Once you're certain you are dealing with a bully, the next step is to determine what your organization has done, if anything, to prevent or prohibit bullying.

In order to begin to determine how (if at all) your organization and workplace bullying intersect, you need to search for any workplace respect, behavior, and/or ethics policies. Take time to investigate. This investigation will determine what options are available to address the problem. It will also impact your action plan goals.

In most large, multi-national and governmental organizations, bullying falls into the broader language of a Workplace Respect Policy or Code of Ethics that stipulates what is considered unacceptable workplace behavior. As background to these policies, particularly in recent years, organizations are constantly striving for better ethical and workplace atmospheres within the business climate and culture. Businesses understand that they must create an ethical and respectful workplace environment in order to develop an ethical and functional organization.

In order to do that, organizations focus on the ethics and behavior of employees in order to create an ethical and respectful workplace. Employees must know the difference between what is acceptable and unacceptable in the workplace. These standards are found in a written Code of Ethics, Workplace Respect Policy or may be referred to as the "Employee Handbook." Your organization may also call these their "Staff Handbook," "Employee Code of Conduct," or the "Company Policy Manual." What the policy is called isn't important – what it says is critical.

These policies lay out the standards in written form of employee conduct and performance expectations. It is important to note that these policies apply to everyone – from the CEO to the support staff. There is no one who is above the policies (or at least that is what the policies clearly state).

Employee handbooks also commonly include rules concerning expectations and consequences that follow misconduct. Handbooks normally will clearly state the rules, guidelines, and standards of an organization as well as possible rules, regulations, and laws that they are bound by. Many company handbooks will include rules and reference applicable laws regarding sexual harassment, alcohol abuse, and drug/substance abuse. For the sake of simplicity, I refer to all of the places where your organization has a written policy on behavioral expectations, including ethics, as "policies."

Regardless of what it's called in your organization, the first step you should take in your investigation is to find your policy and carefully review it. As discussed in more detail in the previous chapter, most policies provide a broad definition of what is considered unacceptable behavior. Usually the definition contains wording like the following:

> *Systematic, annoying, and continued actions that include threats and demands; creating a hostile work situation by uninvited and unwelcome verbal or physical conduct.*

There is no doubt that bullying could fall within the definition of most organizational workplace respect policies. Bullying takes place in a disrespectful workplace and may look and feel like harassment within most of these policies.

The policies normally also provide mechanisms and processes for addressing behavior that violates the policy. They usually have some form of formal complaint process. Reviewing these processes and researching their effectiveness is also helpful. Find out how other complaints have been resolved. The more historical information you have, the better able you are to evaluate your bullying problem. You'll know the risks and rewards of complaining. It will inform you and help you craft your action plan.

One note of warning – in many organizations it isn't obvious that bullying is unacceptable because there isn't a clear policy stating so. Given the overwhelming evidence about the serious impacts caused by bullies, it is difficult to understand why some organizations fail to implement basic workplace respect policies with clear references to bullying. I would even argue it is unethical and negligent. Nonetheless, many people work in places that have failed to grasp the business sense of anti-bullying policies.

Instead of naming it "bullying," some organizations prefer to use more neutral terms. They are shy to give workplace bullying such a direct identifier. I can understand this, but it doesn't help prevent and address the issue when you water it down using less impactful or grey terminology.

With that in mind, I've seen organizations encapsulate bullying behavior within a variety of terms including "workplace disrespect," "unacceptable workplace behavior," "workplace harassment," and "rudeness." While, it may not be ideal, it is still much better than having no behavioral guidelines at all.

Finally, there is the worst-case scenario – organizations that fail to even bother with any policy guiding workplace behavior at all. Leaving such a critical component of workplace culture to develop without any guidelines is highly risky and, in my opinion, foolish. An inclusive, respectful workplace culture is essential for employee engagement and motivation. Leaving such a driver for innovation and performance to chance is negligent and just plain bad for business.

Such organizations also make it almost impossible for both the organization and its employees to take effective action against a bully (or any other bad behavior). Without anything in writing to reference what *is* acceptable behavior, the workplace is basically a behavioral free-for-all. Such organizations are perfect permissive environments for work terrorists – with no accountability structure in place, the workplace is their oyster.

If your organization has behavioral rules in place, dig deeper. Review what the process is for complaining. Research what the historical complaint results have been. Find out if other bullying complaints have been made and what happened. All of this information will help in the action plan decision-making process discussed in detail later on.

If you work in an organization without such policies, the challenges you face when seeking assistance from your organization or attempting to motivate management to take action are very serious. It is essential to be realistic and objectively weigh the likelihood of achieving a positive result from reporting the bully.

***

With the results of your investigation into your organization's workplace behavior policy in hand, you have completed the first step in the process. Now, you can begin to plan your next move. Options to consider are discussed later on.

10

Employer Response and the Effectiveness of Workplace Policies

He that is good for making excuses
is seldom good for anything else.

—Benjamin Franklin[46]

Employer Response Statistics

What happens when organizations are forced to respond to a bullying situation? According to the Workplace Bullying Institute the breakdown of employer responses to reports of workplace bullying is distressing. It paints a disturbing picture that rewards the bully and punishes the victim about 70% of the time.[47]

Employers find a way to deny, rationalize, or discount the severity or even the existence of the problem. "It will resolve itself over time." "Once this very challenging project is over, things will calm down." "We can't afford to deal with this right now but we will after our year-end." "We plan on talking to him in his performance review about his leadership style."

Those are just a sampling of the reasons for inaction. Many organizations also take the position that bullying is really a case of two people who just don't work well together or can't get along. They think the individuals can or should work it out. They may even try to organize a meeting with everyone to "hash things out."

Even more sobering is the fact that many bullies are defended and even encouraged. We've already noted how focusing on results can easily blind executives to how those results are obtained and the poison that is infiltrating the workplace psyche.

The most common resolution of bullying complaints is that the target is punished in one form or another. The target will either leave/quit, be transferred (which is effectively a demotion), be fired, or be forced to quit (perhaps with a severance package). Rare is the organization that takes direct action punishing or terminating the bully. Ironically, in cases where the bully is facing accountability for her actions, it is common for her to quit instead of looking to rehabilitate. This makes perfect sense given the narcissistic tendencies of bullies – emotional intelligence is necessary for humility, remorse, and amends.

If the bully leaves or is forced out, organizations regularly take the position that the problem is solved. In a previous chapter I told a story of a company that fired a vice president bully – well done! However, they promoted the bully's mentor into the position. Bullying isn't like a carpet stain – apply "Bully Be Gone" and it will look just like new. It is a stain that leaves a permanent cultural mark if nothing more is done. Before long, it dawned on the company that they had a copycat bully. Another bully fired – well done! The total cost to the organization would make any CEO cringe.

Often, organizations make no effort to ensure that the workplace culture is re-focused, reassured, and given a chance to recover. It takes time and engagement from management to heal a broken work environment. In one situation, after the bully departed, the unit continued to bleed talent, for months and even years later. There continued to be a sense of fear, a lack of team spirit and general malaise that permeated the unit. From an outsider's perspective it was so obvious why the losses continued, yet no one on the inside did anything.

It takes little investment to ensure those left behind are given an opportunity to process, discuss, and shed their shattered levels of engagement. Like a death in the family, the emotional elephant in the room only gets bigger and the scars rarely heal without compassion and communication.

What about the Workplace Respect Policy?

As already noted in Chapter 9, many organizations have some form of Respectful Workplace Policy, Code of Ethics, or Employee Handbook laying out the expected guidelines for employee behavior. Most policies provide a broad definition of what is considered unacceptable behavior. Bullying is usually a policy violation, at least on paper.

I applaud any organization that sets down guidelines for unacceptable workplace behavior. However, organizations must consistently and assertively apply the policy. Workplace respect policies are only as effective as the commitment from organizations to enforce them and leaders to align with them. They must respond fairly and effectively to violation allegations. Complaints can't be shrugged off lightly or interpreted as two employees who can't get along.

In other words, the leaders must "walk the walk" and follow through by demonstrating that the policy is valued and enforced. I've heard many hollow clichés about organizations that allegedly view their employees as their most valuable asset yet do nothing when it comes to demonstrating real leadership in the case of workplace bullies.

Sharon told me her government department had a very clear and strongly worded workplace respect policy. It even referenced bullying directly. Her bully had been with the organization for over a decade and everyone working there knew about her boss's well-deserved reputation as a bully. However, when she filed a very carefully worded, well-documented bullying complaint, she was treated as if she was a trouble-maker. She was thrown under the bus – the human resources manager promptly informed her boss, leading to an intolerable escalation of bullying. Sharon ended up having a heart attack. Thankfully, she recovered and left the organization. Those left behind were also devastated and, one by one, everyone who could, moved on to more harmonious places. So much for that respectful workplace policy!

As evidenced by Sharon's experience, it is also important to appreciate that workplace respect policies are internal to organizations. Therefore, if an employee is accused of violating the policy, it is managed exclusively from within. Any investigation, resolution, or punishment is a corporate affair. This further underlines why it is important to send consistent and clear messaging to all staff and follow through.

The internal reality of workplace respect policies also highlights their weakness. The vast majority of executives and managers are afraid to engage the bully in a confrontation about their behavior. They also lack awareness and training in how to successfully approach the problem. Furthermore, there is rarely anyone they can turn to for advice.

In most organizations, the human resource staff and managers lack specific training or skills for dealing with bullies. When management turns to them for help, they regularly provide the wrong recommendations. They believe influencers can reason with a bully and that once they have expressed their concerns, things will improve. This is entirely ineffective and usually accelerates the bullying behavior.

Human resources and the senior executives are also usually reluctant to bring in external experts to help resolve the problem, even though many of them are available. This is an admission of the seriousness of the problem they are unwilling to make. It also involves cost and accountability – once they have a report and recommended action plan from such experts, they must take action. They prefer to handle the matter "in-house" with results that rarely eliminate the bullying.

Furthermore, as will be discussed in later chapters, normal complaint, investigation, and conflict resolution processes used in most organizations aren't effective with bullies. The most common process directs employees to lodge a complaint with their supervisor. When bullies are the bosses most of the time, it's easy to see why this fails to resolve the problem.

Without the appropriate specialized training and procedures, targets that complain usually get little satisfaction from the matter. The internal system is stacked against effective resolution.

***

Employers aren't exactly rushing to stop bullying at work when it occurs. The most common resolution is that the bully is managed while the target is punished. This has to change. I believe that if we all play our part in a global "workplace bully disruption" movement, the status quo will positively improve over time.

Despite their good intentions and best efforts, many organizations fail to protect themselves and their employees when they initiate respectful workplace policies and programs. The bullies use their talent for manipulation, deceit, and counter-attack to turn the process into another opportunity to bully. Chapter 12 examines ways that organizations can take charge in a bullying situation and protect not only the bottom line, but also the integrity of the organization.

11

Why Are Organizations So Ineffective at Managing Bullying?

Management is doing things right;
leadership is doing the right things.

—Peter Drucker[48]

Bullying is sufficiently understood and so prevalent that most employers should be prepared to effectively handle it. However, despite laws, irrefutable data and research, and ethical reasons to do so, most organizations are generally very unprepared. They haven't yet come to appreciate the costs of not acting or the most effective ways to confront the problem. Senior management say, "People are our most valuable asset," but that is often a hollow cliché when it comes to bullying.

Zogby Analytics was commissioned to conduct an online survey of 315 U.S. business leaders in three market areas: San Francisco, New York City, and Washington D.C. The survey was completed January 21, 2013.[49] The leaders were asked the following question:

> *Which of the following best describes your opinion of "workplace bullying"?*

The answers were enlightening. The percentages for each response option were:

- *68% agreed – It is a serious problem.*
- *17% answered – I have never heard of it.*
- *15% said – It is irrelevant, a non-issue, bullying affects only children.*

If so many business leaders think bullying is a serious problem, why are most organizations terrible at managing it? There are many contributors to fully answer this question. Often more than one factor is involved. It helps to identify the most common reasons. They include, but aren't limited to, the following:

Employers Are Afraid to Confront Bullies

Fear is what I commonly refer to when I publicly speak about workplace bullying as the elephant in the room. I've heard far too many stories about senior management pretending there is no issue and making terrible decisions in relation to a well-known workplace bully problem.

I believe fear is the number-one reason why our leaders fail to enforce their own policies related to workplace respect and bullying. While most leaders are aware of workplace bullying and that it is a severe problem, many organizations lack the training, tools, policies, and expertise to confront it. More importantly, they are afraid to step into the ring with the bully. They lack the courage to take action. Bullying is a sensitive topic because it requires confrontation, conflict, and bravery as much as it requires tools.

Fear often feeds into the ignorance: fear of lawsuits, of the actual confrontation with the bully, of what else might be uncovered once an investigation is launched, of how many other victims might be in the organization. All of these fears are real and fair but they don't justify a failure to act.

Having talked with plenty of executives and HR personnel, it is fair to state that fear of conflict is a serious impediment to eliminating bullying. The result is that management walks on eggshells and is afraid to confront the "golden" bully. While HR does its best to deal with the complaints, conflicts, and impacts, the result is paralysis – and so the bullying continues.

However, there is a lost opportunity cost of doing nothing and, as has already been discussed, that cost is dear. Performance, productivity, and other ripple effects resonate throughout the organization. The bully continues to wreak havoc and this won't stop until the organization takes action – to get the guts to confront the bully. Those who don't act could be directly impacted by their inaction – they could lose their job, their reputation, their career.

If you're a leader reading this book, I implore you to think hard about your responsibility for enforcing your organization's policies – it isn't a negotiable commitment, but rather a fundamental duty that you owe to your employees, your organization, and yourself. Your personal integrity and ethical values are at stake. Are you going to choose the high road, protecting those you lead and holding those behaving badly accountable? Are you prepared to show courage, confront your fear, and do the right thing? It is your response to these questions that will distinguish you as a trustworthy leader (or not).

A Focus on Results

In our hyper-competitive world there is intense and ever-present demands for results. Many organizations become so focused on short-term results that they ignore how they are achieved or the long-term impacts of the means used to get those results. Organizations willingly sacrifice a harmonious workplace culture in order to please shareholders, customers, and stakeholders with baseline results. They may believe their employees matter most but in actual fact, results trump everything.

Sadly, this focal point is candy for bullies. If there is one commonality amongst bullies, it's a gift for whipping up results (and those used to get them). Later on, when organizations see the fallout from the bully, they realize the price they paid for those results far exceeds the benefits reaped from them.

Through increased awareness and focusing on the costs associated with bullying, there is hope that even when faced with pressure to perform, organizations will forbid bullying as a results-driver. In the meantime, the stories of bullying will continue.

Misinterpretation of a "Competitive Workplace"

Many organizations confuse healthy competition with a "survival of the fittest" model for workplace behavior. High tech is infamous for condoning bullying, viewing it as normal behavior in a competitive workplace. There have been stories (and articles, books, and movies) about Amazon, Apple, and other companies where staff is regularly challenged to out-perform and out-innovate their colleagues using draconian rewards for the winner.

Some argue bullies manage these organizations, which is why the workplace culture is so Darwinian (an entirely reasonable assertion). To quote Orrin Woodward, founder of Life Leadership and bestselling author: "You cannot expect your team to rise above your example."[50]

If we assume that the CEO isn't a bully, I believe there is a lack of appreciation of the direct relationship between employee engagement and workplace culture. If there are rewards for cutthroat competition and the workplace culture resembles the set of the TV reality series *Survivor*, there is little chance for workplace respect. Bullies will thrive and there will be very little employee loyalty and engagement.

It is my hypothesis that leaders fail to understand that it is possible (and in the best long-term organizational interest) to have both workplace respect and healthy competition. Staff don't need to be abused to perform to their fullest.

A Belief that Bullying Is a Leadership Style

This false connection has already been discussed in a previous chapter. Bullying is the opposite of leadership. In my opinion, executives who use this excuse to support a bully are likely in denial or afraid to confront the problem. If asked in a moment of unbridled honesty, they likely know exactly who the abusers are. They just don't have the skills or motivation to take action so they leave the mess alone, hoping it will sort itself out. They discount the level of the problem, rationalize it as a temporary issue, blame it on a very challenging time, or find another excuse to avoid actively engaging.

Lack of Awareness about Workplace Bullying

As hard as it seems to accept, there remains a small segment of leadership that has yet to become enlightened on the topic of workplace bullying. What's even more surprising is that their ignorance may be genuine. Rather than judge the poorly informed, it may be more useful to see their lack of awareness as an opportunity to empower them with knowledge. If they are simply acting out of willful blindness, there is a lack of leadership ethics and accountability at the core of the problem.

Lack of Effective Policies and Processes

It is remarkable how few organizations actually have taken all the evidence, information, and advice of experts about workplace bullying to heart. Whatever the reason for their inaction, there is a lack of effective policies and processes for dealing with bullying. For example, without a workplace respect policy (or similar), it is very difficult to frame the approach to addressing a bully situation. On the other hand, if the organization has a robustly worded policy, the base from which to respond to a bully is well-founded.

Not only are the policies essential, but also the processes for actually managing bullying issues. Without a fair, impartial, confidential, and effective complaints process, the policy is meaningless. How does an organization expect to deal properly with bullying if the complaint process requires a formal written complaint to the supervisor? Lest we forget that bullies are statistically most often the supervisor to whom the complaint would have to be made. It is also helpful to remember that no alleged bully should be presumed guilty without due process. Thus, the process is essential to defensible and trustworthy outcomes.

Further, it is equally difficult if the human resources department is considered the best place for the complaint management. This is neither neutral nor fair for anyone involved, including the HR professionals. Organizations need a complaints process staffed with trained people who understand the challenges of dealing with bullying. That unit requires the authority to create a process that is managed by unbiased, bully-trained investigators who have ample authority to carry out an investigation. This includes the power to interview anyone they deem appropriate and to be provided access to the workplace and people in order to do this difficult job.

Often, the best means to achieve this end is to establish a relationship with a consulting firm that has both the expertise and lack of bias to do this work. They have no pre-conceived notions, nothing at risk, and, provided they can do their job free from influence and intervention, this is a superb choice of process.

Finally, the investigators must have recommendation-making authority and there must be proper conflict resolution processes available to effectively manage the next steps. Using standard models for dealing with normal conflicts doesn't work with bullying. The process must be fair to all and the investigators must be able to make binding decisions.

Lack of Trained HR/Staff

Despite their best efforts and good intentions, many HR personnel are unprepared or lack the authority to address bullies. They are also limited by the policies in their work-place. If those policies are weak or ineffective, so will HR's efforts to address the problem.

Human resource professionals also face a difficult choice – they have the organization's best interests as their priority but they usually see what is really going on. Often, they want to take action against the bully but they don't have the training, authority, or capacity to do so. They are also often prevented from seeking external experts to assist. The result is that they fail the organization and, unintentionally, contribute to the problem.

This plays out to the benefit of the bully and the detri-ment of the target. Most of the time, the moment a target rais-es the bullying flag to HR, they respond with fear and think about the organization's protection. Usually that means they view the complaint as a threat to the company, a liability, a lawsuit waiting to happen, and a PR nightmare in the shad-ows. As professionals working for the company, they go into risk-management mode, often seeking advice from legal, and likely developing an exit strategy for the target. In effect, they focus all their effort on managing the target and protecting the bully.

Most organizations haven't grasped that HR staff aren't prepared or trained to deal with bullies. None of the standard conflict management strategies are effective because you can't reason with bullies. People tend to believe that they can persuade, apply logic, or collaboratively resolve bullying conflicts. This ignores the sociopathic nature of bullies and the genesis of their motivation.

***

The above are the main reasons why organizations fail to respond effectively to bullying situations. There are undoubtedly others that I have failed to mention. What is important is that even though the vast majority of leaders acknowledge bullying is a very serious problem and should be eradicated, very few actually do.

12

Changing Employer Behavior: An Organizational Anti-bullying Action Plan

A man without ethics is a wild beast loosed upon this world.

—Albert Camus[51]

Now that we know bullying is bad for business and there are many arguments for eliminating bullying. Let's shift the focus to motivating change and inspiring hope. Governments are slowly responding and initiating profound change. If there are anti-bullying laws in effect, every organization should take action to ensure they are in compliance with the law. Even then, mere compliance shouldn't be the goal – instead a sincere desire to change and create a workplace culture that motivates and inspires everyone should drive the anti-bullying movement.

Regardless of whether governments have yet to take action, it is reassuring that every organization can take action that will have tremendous permanent impact. There are experts to help, training and tools that are readily available, and a lot of online resources to guide the way. It requires investment, committed leadership, and a sincere desire to implement change. However, the investment is small compared to the risk that organizations are eliminating.

Throughout the world, business-savvy organizations are taking increasingly preventative steps to confront workplace bullying, reinforcing their ethical awareness and instilling confidence in employees and those who do business with them. It is far better to proactively and directly address the bullying than to permit spreading poison throughout the organization.

There are a host of proactive and preventative measures that motivated organizations can take. Some of the most practical, proactive tips are the following:

a) Establish or revise Respectful Workplace and Ethics Policies

Create organizational codes of ethics and respectful workplace policies that clearly include anti-bullying policies, effective methods to report and investigate bad behavior, and make annual training for workplace ethics and respect mandatory. All organizations should establish clear and effective bullying policies and procedures for addressing bullying allegations. If your organization has no anti-bullying policy, staff and managers should lobby hard for change.

b) Initiate awareness campaigns

As noted earlier, there remains a lack of awareness regarding workplace bullying. Many people lack the tools and knowledge to identify bullies and understand the situation once a bully has been identified. Thus, it is essential that everyone in the organization be provided with baseline information and a bully-awareness tool kit.

Senior management must lead the awareness campaign, showing authentic engagement. Their level of involvement provides a strong message for staff and managers. This isn't just the ethical and right thing to do – it's good for business. By taking leadership on this issue, executives are also showing true leadership behavior. There's self-interest to motivate you to take the reins of change.

c) Invest in training

Training, awareness, and education are critical to the success of such policies. Human resources must be on board and not feel unprepared. Each segment of the organization requires training adapted for the audience. Executives and leaders have different responsibilities and points of focus than do employees.

d) Walk the walk

There is no replacement for authentic, engaged leadership. Just like any important initiative, unless everyone witnesses sincere, meaningful, and consistent anti-bullying messages and behavior from the executives, the goal will never be reached. It may be cliché, but to eliminate bullying the change must come from and be led by example from the top.

From the CEO and senior managers all the way down to lower-ranking staff, the message must be direct, consistent, and clear – there is zero tolerance for bullying. Even the slightest hint that it might be tolerated is often enough for a bully to cause damage.

e) Demonstrate ethical leadership and accountability

All organizations, through the actions of their leaders, have a direct impact on organizational success, reputation, employees, industry, and society. Organizations can't allow their leaders to participate in decisions or actions that are immoral or against the basic judgement of right and wrong.

In effect, organizations must demand that their leaders hold themselves and, thus, their organization to the highest standards of ethical behavior. Further, organizations must be crystal clear that executives will be held accountable for upholding the duties they owe to their organization. Finally, they must be vigilant for ethical breaches and take decisive action when they arise.

f) Improve performance management strategies

One of the most effective ways to improve organizational workplace culture is to include performance metrics for respectful behavior and attitude in performance plans for every employee. Give managers a tool to directly address bad behavior the moment it surfaces. By making the employees accountable for disrespectfulness, organizations increase the impact of their workplace respect policies.

g) Implement fair reporting processes

Establish fair, effective, and safe methods to report alleged bullying: Bullying isn't like other conflicts in the workplace. It requires specialized processes and methods for conflict resolution. First, an unbiased, safe, and user-friendly complaint-reporting process is essential. This works to everyone's benefit and will ensure impartial, confidential, and trustworthy processes.

h) Establish investigation processes

Bullying investigations must be impartial, fair, and fulsome. In order for a staff to feel safe and have faith that their employer takes this issue seriously, it is essential that investigations are unbiased, confidential, free from political interference, and result in appropriate responses if allegations are proven. An impartial investigator should be engaged to conduct this sensitive work and be permitted to speak to anyone who may have witnessed the activity. Fair treatment for all alleged victims, bullies, and witnesses is needed to engender trust in the process.

i) Take all bullying reports seriously

Take bullying claims seriously but tread carefully. Until there has been a thorough assessment of the complaint by unbiased and trained personnel, the organization should remain neutral. The important point here is that organizations should respond immediately and professionally.

While every report of bullying or bullying-type behavior should be taken seriously, whether they have merit is for the investigation process to determine. It is fair to say that some allegations will turn out to be situations that involve conflict between two competitive staff, or misunderstandings, or communication breakdowns. Regardless, the investigation will provide the organization with a neutral report that helps senior management address the problem, whatever it turns out to be.

j) Use effective conflict resolution strategies

Normal conflict resolution processes won't work with bullies: It is naïve to think that you can reason with a bully. Holding a meeting with the bully to "hash out" management's concerns will usually result in the bully defending their actions, using deceit, blame, and deflection as their primary means to convince management the problem lies with the target. In other words, there will be no progress, no accountability.

The most common next step is the bully will take out even greater revenge on the target, assuming she/he is responsible for ratting on the bully. The net result from management's attempt to reason is that life for the target gets progressively worse.

Furthermore, mediation is simply another opportunity for the bully to misbehave and instill fear in the target. This is an organizational problem that requires impactful decision-making authority, not a compromise-seeking session. Thus binding arbitration is normally the best process to use. Often, the organization will find it doesn't get this far.

***

With all of these policies and processes in place, there is no guarantee that your organization won't ever face a bullying situation. However, when it happens, the organization will be prepared to handle the challenges effectively, with due process. If there is a bully in the midst, there are mechanisms for quickly snuffing out the problem. Bullies beware – change is coming!

13

Individual Engagement: Laying the Foundation for Your Anti-Bullying Action Plan

You get what you expect and deserve what you tolerate.

—Mark Graban,[52]
author and healthcare expert

We've discussed how our organizations can take action to implement change and improve the status quo for their response to workplace bullies. Let's now shift the focus to what each of us, as individuals, can do to be a critical part of the movement to change how we respond to the same bullies.

Before providing specific action plans for different people depending on their role and relationship to the workplace bully, there are some essential markers that apply to everyone. These are the foundation and pillars upon which all individual anti-bullying action plans are built. Regardless of where you work, your job title, or your relationship to the bully, every person will be more successful in bully management if they ensure they have a well-built behavioral foundation. This foundation will also help us in our relationships, managing conflicts in both our career and personal success.

In crafting the foundation, it's important to remind ourselves that regardless of your title, you have influence, you are a leader and your actions have impact. It may seem (and may very well be accurate) that you have little power or no decision-making authority to take the kind of action that might be needed to effectively eliminate a bully. However, to say that you are powerless or without influence is untrue.

There are always things you can do, always options that you can exercise. It will take courage. It will take patience. It will take planning. It will be difficult. But, taking power away from the bully and focusing on your action plan changes the dynamic at play – from being a victim, a witness, a bystander, or, in my view, the worst way to address bullying, an ostrich, to taking action, starting a movement, using your influence and showing real leadership.

The "cement" of your foundation requires the following components, each of which I deal with separately;

a) An awareness of your leadership style;
b) An awareness of the road blocks that inhibit you from acting;
c) An understanding of the consequences of silence;
d) A willingness to have "fierce conversations"; and
e) A sound self-accountability framework.

a) An Awareness of Your Leadership Style

The first building block for your action plan to address a workplace bully is a deep awareness of your personal leadership style and a willingness to change it if you realize it isn't serving you well. Each of us establishes and fosters workplace behavior expectations through our own leadership values and actions. Simply put – we learn from the examples set by those above, and those around us learn from how we lead.

Remember – we are *all leaders*. In effect, that leads to

two clear choices that each of us have: Do you commit to a positive servant leadership model for workplace culture or a "command and control" model? This fundamental decision impacts your organization, your colleagues, your teams, and it also reflects back onto you as a leader. It directly impacts your reputation and whether people trust and believe in your integrity.

Professor Edwin Locke, an industrial psychologist, defines Leadership as *the process of inducing others to pursue a common goal or vision.* Locke's definition focuses on two key components: formulating a shared goal or vision; and persuading others to follow. Leadership then is an activity with an overarching purpose – to inspire others to act in the pursuit of a joint value or set of values. Leadership is also a relational concept – without followers, there cannot be a leader.

There are many ways to lead (and to approach dealing with a bully), and these are commonly referred to as "leadership styles." I'm not simply referring to personal style or personality type, but to a broader set of approaches and attributes discussed below. The two most commonly debated leadership styles are "servant leadership" and "command and control."

Let's begin by reviewing each of the most oft-mentioned leadership styles:

Servant Leadership

The basic premise for servant leadership is that the leader is there to serve his or her people. In formulating a vision, the leader seeks participation and approval from them and the main approach to pursuing the vision lies in removing obstacles and helping followers be successful.

While servant leadership is a timeless concept, the phrase "servant leadership" was coined by Robert K. Greenleaf in "The Servant as Leader," an essay that he first published in 1970. In that essay, Greenleaf said:

> *The servant-leader is servant first... It begins with the natural feeling that one wants to serve, to serve first. Then conscious choice brings one to aspire to lead...The difference manifests itself in the care taken by the servant-first to make sure that other people's highest priority needs are being served. The best test, and difficult to administer, is: Do those served grow as persons? Do they, while being served, become healthier, wiser, freer, more autonomous, more likely themselves to become servants?*[53]

Servant leadership is probably the most prevalent leadership style in modern industry. It works on the principle that the people we employ and work with have the benefit of education, professional skills, and experience. Organizational leaders empower them to use these tools and talents to make decisions on their behalf. It's a "*do as you see fit*" style of leadership.

Command-and-control leadership

Command-and-control leadership is based on establishing and maintaining power over, and control of, people and organizational processes. This style, often associated with the military, emphasizes a strict chain of command with hierarchies of goals and limited autonomy. It is an authoritarian regime where one person holds absolute power and responsibility for the organization and people.

Command and control is a common leadership style. Many of today's leaders were mentored themselves by command-and-control managers, and the culture of a lot of organizations is still based on command-and-control norms. It is hard to escape this leadership style's historic influence and dominance.

This enables total coordination and accountability for their subordinates. This is a "*do exactly as I say*" model. The leader makes orders. The people serve the leader. There is no room for debate and there are serious consequences for non-compliance.

Some argue this style of leadership is appropriate for tasks and projects where there are uncomplicated simple tasks with little room for human error. On the surface, this sounds like a good idea: You certainly don't want people's behavior or steps in your change process to be "out of control." A good example of this might be a car factory or food plants where conveyor belts and other machinery are utilized.

Choosing a Servant Leadership Model

When you, in your daily approach to being a leader, walk the walk of servant leadership, there are direct benefits to the workplace culture. Servant leadership creates a positive, respectful workplace and the benefits to the bottom line in terms of employee motivation, productivity, engagement, loyalty, and innovation are exponential. Human resources professionals also report that a harmonious workplace culture contributes to improvements in employee turnover, sick leave reduction, and lower benefits costs.

Choosing a servant leadership model will also result in a critical component of effective leadership – trust. This is not only my opinion but has been underscored by some of the most important thought leaders of our time. *The Leadership Challenge* by Kouzes and Posner is the gold standard for research-based leadership and is a premier resource for aspiring leaders. The text informs us that leadership requires trust: "It's clear that if people anywhere are to willingly follow someone – whether it be into battle or into the boardroom, the front office or the front lines – they first want to assure themselves that the person is worthy of their trust."[54]

There are many examples of leaders that authentically embody servant leadership values. Warren Buffet and Bill Gates, two of the world's most respected and recognized business leaders, represent the servant leadership perspective that a positive workplace culture based on values that include workplace respect, ethics, and accountability lead to profitability. In an interesting YouTube video related to ethics and profitability, Mr. Buffet comments: "You can succeed magnificently with ethics. It's not a hindrance… There is no reason to cut corners."[55]

Sam Walton, co-founder of Wal-Mart is another icon of corporate success that vigorously supports a servant leadership model. "Outstanding leaders go out of their way to boost the self-esteem of their personnel. If people believe in themselves, it's amazing what they can accomplish."[56]

Choosing a Command-and-Control Model

Leaders who choose a command-and-control model drive predominantly through dominance, fear, and negative reinforcement. Employees have no choice but to do as their leader says. One can see the merit of this leadership style on the battlefield. However, I don't believe it belongs in the workplace.

Here's why. Command and control as a leadership style destroys virtually any chance for a high-performance workplace culture. Fear isn't a positive motivator. It reduces employee engagement and commitment, and often actually promotes resistance. It results in lost productivity, creativity, and loyalty. I'm not alone in my assessment. In their 2014 article, Dan Ackerman and Linda Ackerman Anderson found that a command and control leadership style impedes organizational success.[57] In particular, they found that it causes transformational change efforts to fail.

The command-and-control model creates a workplace culture where employees feel vulnerable, anxious, and uncertain. All too commonly, leaders who choose this model also tolerate disrespectful behavior. They motivate by threat, humiliation, and exerting power over others.

I believe that when leaders tolerate disrespect or behave that way themselves, those underneath them will adopt the same approach. The result is a "monkey-see monkey-do" workplace. Following their leader's disrespectful lead, senior management will say "People are our most valuable asset," but that will be a hollow cliché. The workplace culture will resonate disrespect, creating a Darwinian workplace – if survival of the fittest is what the leader desires, then that is likely what will eventually happen.

There are examples of leaders who have adopted command-and-control leadership styles. Jeff Bezos of Amazon and Don Blankenship of Massey Mines are two high-profile adoptees. In a *60 Minutes* exposé, the program explains how Don Blankenship ended up in prison for ordering staff to ignore safety regulations, which ultimately led to the death of coal miners working at Massey Mines. This is a sad and extreme example of the negative impact of a bully running an organization using a command and control leadership style.[58]

In an interesting 2017 article in the *New York Times*, the writers suggest that Amazon exemplifies the impact of Mr. Bezos' deliberate choice of leadership style and workplace culture. The article aptly points out that Bezos' strategy may in fact be producing diabolical long-term impacts on reputation, innovation, disengagement, and turnover that other leaders should consider. Mr. Bezos is "getting what he expects and deserves what he tolerates."[59] Following this logic, leading by exerting power and workplace disrespect creates a disrespectful culture. Fear will be the primary motivator. The article alleges that is exactly how things work at Amazon.

By highlighting the pitfalls of leading using command-and-control tactics of negative reinforcement, bullying, and disrespect, I hope to inspire you to choose to embrace a respectful workplace culture by adopting a servant leadership approach.

Workplace Bullying – The Leadership Style Test

There is irrefutable data that the attitude and approach to leadership that you bring to work each day sets the tone and behavioral expectations for your coworkers and organizations – your leadership style, expectations, and workplace respect tolerance levels ripple throughout the business. In our hyper-competitive world there are intense and ever-present demands for results. Many organizations become so focused on short-term results that they ignore how they are achieved or the long-term impacts of the means used to get those results.

I believe each of us determine our destiny when we choose our leadership values and style. The choice is quite simple – do ego/results/profits alone drive the workplace culture or does workplace culture drive results/profits? There are incredibly successful leaders who vehemently oppose the command and control leadership style.

Through increased awareness and focusing on the costs associated with a fear-driven workplace culture, I hope that, despite constant pressure to perform, you will cease using command-and-control leadership as a results-driver. I hope that you will show courage and walk the talk of servant leadership. In the meantime, the stories of leaders that select command and control continue to educate us about the consequences (including at Volkswagen,[60] FIFA,[61] and a host of others). Further, reports of leaders paying a dear price for their choice of leadership values will also continue.

To quote Orrin Woodward, founder of Life Leadership and bestselling author: "*You cannot expect your team to rise above your example.*"[62] To choose or not to choose (a respectful servant leadership style) – that is the leader's question. What you choose will have a tremendous impact on your effectiveness in addressing bad behavior at work.

b) An Awareness of the Roadblocks that Inhibit You from Taking Action

Without self-awareness, we are as babies in the cradles.

—Virginia Woolf[63]

The second building block for our action plan to address a workplace bully is a commitment to increase our awareness of our personality flaws that prevent us from being effective. Each of us has what I refer to as personal "roadblocks" that inhibit us from taking action against workplace bullies. Roadblocks create a form of paralysis that prevents us from confronting the problem, even when we know that we should.

These roadblocks usually represent "black holes" in our self-awareness. Our moral compass points north towards action but our roadblocks point south, rendering us incapable of doing what we know is the "right" thing to do.

The only way we can begin addressing our roadblocks is to acknowledge, first, that they are there and, second, what they actually are. In working with many organizations, I've seen a profound lack of roadblock awareness in many training sessions and workshops. If we don't even know there is a roadblock ahead, we can't begin breaking it down. For example, if we look in the mirror and see a self-confident, assertive person but the true reflection is a frightened, vulnerable person, our warped self-perception creates all kinds of daily problems, particularly when we are faced with emotional challenges. Thus, in order to remove our roadblocks, we must start by improving our self-awareness.

The lesson learned is that we can't assume each of us, our coworkers, or our executives have sufficient self-awareness to understand why they are paralyzed in fear, doubt, and silence when confronted with a workplace bully. It's easy to blame their ineffectiveness or inaction on a lack of accountability, poor leadership, and a shirking of responsibility (which may be fair in certain situations).

However, if those who should act are oblivious as to why they don't respond and lack awareness of the roadblocks that prevent them from getting involved, the basis for their inaction is different – it's not fair to focus on their lack of moral fiber or accountability. Instead, we must try to educate them and help them understand the root of their motivation to do nothing. They need our support and for us to hold them accountable for developing tools to break their roadblock patterns. It's up to them to commit to their personal growth. It's only when they choose not to act, with full knowledge of their flaws, that I believe we should raise the lack of leadership and failed accountability flags.

I've identified five primary roadblocks that make us ineffective at addressing workplace bullying. These roadblocks will also prevent us from dealing with a family argument, a disagreement with your boss or colleague, a poorly behaved child, a rude store attendant, or a corrupt government official. In simple terms, roadblocks get in our way in all facets of life. Overcoming them will make us better people leading more enjoyable lives.

My roadblock list isn't exhaustive, but I believe that it represents the most common problems that render us ineffective when confronted with a workplace bully. I will address each one separately:

Roadblock 1: A Negative Attitude

A bad attitude is like a flat tire. You can't go anywhere until you change it.

—Unknown[64]

Also known as "the blame game," negativity creates inertia, bringing not only the person with the bad attitude down, but she drags down those around her too. It's certainly easier to point a finger at others as the source of the problem or the person who has responsibility for fixing an issue. However, the effort involved in choosing to be a positive influence significantly outweighs the cons of negativity.

If you choose to approach life and its challenges through the lens of negativity, I can assure you that a workplace bully will run circles around you. Bullies will use your attitude as a tool to manipulate you. They may encourage you to gossip about the person they are targeting, knowing that with the right information, your attitude will drive you to do their dirty work. In effect, your negativity may make you an ally for a bully that you despise. Alternatively, the bully may then heighten your negativity, making you feel worse, more vulnerable, and more powerless. For example, if you're friends with those the bully targets, the bully may also target you, capitalizing on your bad attitude.

For leaders in our organizations, it is useful to remind ourselves that negativity impacts workplace culture, team engagement, and impedes both innovation and success. Those who are negative are commonly those who enjoy gossip and stirring up conflict. If the response to everything that isn't working is "no," "that's not my job," "this will never change," "she did that," "our systems make it impossible to do that," or hundreds of other negatives, I encourage leaders to push back.

One way that I approach negativity is to create a ground rule with staff and teams for how we approach a challenge (as opposed to a problem). I'm absolutely interested in hearing about issues that are impeding personal or team success. However, I insist that if you can identify a problem, then you can also identify a number of possible solutions to fix it. I allow teams limited time to complain and have a great deal of patience for their collaborative efforts to resolve a challenge. Potential solutions have to be practical and reasonable – something that is financially manageable or within my scope of control as a leader. While it takes perseverance and tolerance, I've used this approach effectively to slowly bring those on the dark side back to the positive.

For those of us who tend towards the negative, I encourage you to spend as much time talking about the problem as talking about how you can be part of the solution. I promise you that it's more empowering to be in control of your destiny as opposed to relying on everyone to run your life and fix your issues. I realize that you will likely face the dreaded and inevitable concept of change. However, if you can become the change driver as opposed to the person who is "being forced" to change, you will quickly discover that life is much better on the positive side of issues.

For those of us who have colleagues who are negative, I challenge you to hold them accountable for their poor attitude. Insist that their job responsibilities include engaging in problem solving and not just problem identification. If your coworker continues to whine, blame, and gossip, set a boundary that you won't engage in a discussion with them until they can be constructive and are willing to own their part of the problem. Isolate the negativity – this approach usually is contagious. Lead by example and soon those who are as fed up with negativity as you will join you in setting expected standards of behavior.

Negativity is a road block that makes you unlikeable as a colleague, vulnerable to being ignored, and puts you in the bully's crosshairs. We can all play a role in dealing with our own negativity and holding others accountable when they get negative.

Roadblock 2: Awareness Blind Spots

We all have blind spots – those areas for improvement and growth. As painful as it can be to admit we're doing things we never wanted to do and saying things we never wanted to say, it is this acknowledgement that enables us to take the first step toward change. Be gentle with yourself. Be real with yourself. Take baby steps.

—Rhonda Louise Robbins,[65]
Author

We are impacted by those around us, where and how we grew up, our cultural background, and a myriad of other factors that create our perspectives on the world. One of our challenges is that our lenses create roadblocks in the form of natural biases, stereotypes, and uninformed judgement of others. It can also warp our perception of who we believe we are and how we think others view us. How many times have we advised a coworker that they hurt another's feelings and heard the response from him that "I had no idea that I was being insensitive" or "I don't understand how that is offensive"?

I refer to this roadblock as our awareness blind spots. They are normal; we all have them. They aren't bad or good (but they can be). It's one thing to have a natural bias on a particular topic or in relation to a person – we are entitled to our opinions. However, if that bias is blinding us to the point that we are stereotyping or drawing unfair conclusions about that topic or person, therein lies the problem.

For example, Bhupinder believed that when he interacted with younger female colleagues he was fair and appropriate. In fact, he was condescending and patronizing. He had no awareness that he treated them in a way that offended them. When this issue was raised, at first, he was sincerely shocked. However, over the course of the discussion he began to appreciate that he had a cultural blind spot – he came from both a male-dominated home and culture. Boys were given preferential treatment and girls were "less than" boys.

Bullies tend to have little-to-no awareness of their blind spots. Even if they are self-aware, they honestly don't care that they are stereotyping or unfairly judging others. Furthermore, they are adept at social manipulation and may take advantage of your blind spots if it will help them. Using the case of Bhupinder as an example, a bully who is targeting one of his female coworkers would likely confirm that his biases are correct and encourage him to speak his mind, thereby assisting the bully in making her feel less than, isolated, and vulnerable. Much like the case of negativity, your lack of awareness can position you to be used as a bully's tool.

Provided we are emotionally mature and have a desire to continuously improve, we can overcome our awareness blind spots. We can learn to curiously engage with the world, seeking to enhance our limited knowledge and exposure to those who are different from us. From an awareness of our biases we can catch ourselves when we begin to judge or stereotype. We can enhance our diversity intelligence and evolve into better people.

In the case of Bhupinder, he worked out a feedback plan where his colleagues provided constructive help and he was encouraged to ask them questions. His sincere desire to personally grow and the willingness of his coworkers to assist without judging him created the ideal relationship-building environment. Everyone benefited and learned a great deal from each other about their uniqueness.

Awareness blind spots are like any other blind spot – they create risk and can cause unfortunate accidents. They can tear apart a team, a relationship, an organization. They can also make you a target for bully manipulation. However, with a willingness to grow and improve, they can be overcome as in the case of Bhupinder.

Roadblock 3: Communication Barriers

The single biggest problem in communication is the illusion that is has taken place.

—George Bernard Shaw[66]

Without question, the most common source of conflict of all kinds is a breakdown in communication. There are hundreds of books and experts that you can turn to for assistance with addressing communication barriers of all types. I won't try to do justice to their body of work. In the context of roadblocks that prevent us from effectively taking action against a workplace bully, communication barriers are an all too common problem. They are also used by bullies as a mechanism to drive deeper wedges between people and ignite conflicts.

Although the list below is far from exhaustive, in my experience, this represents some of the most common forms of communication barriers. I haven't described them in detail and have left that for you to explore.

- Inter-generational communication challenges;
- Language and cultural issues;
- Educational barriers (different professions, training and backgrounds);
- Sexual and racial barriers (sexual orientation, racial differences);
- Organizational barriers (time, hierarchy, location); and
- Emotional barriers (fear, anxiety, shyness).

If there are roadblocks preventing us from communicating effectively, it's very easy to misunderstand, offend, create confusion, and unintentionally create conflict. Workplace bullies are adept at using communication barriers to introduce chaos and conflicts. They also take advantage of our barriers, using them as a spear to hurt, ridicule, humiliate.

Luisa told me that her workplace bully regularly mocked her accent from El Salvador and would imitate her in meetings.

It is up to each of us to work on improving our communication skills and strive to overcome the barriers that prevent us from ensuring that we are understood, respected, and respectful.

Roadblock 4: Comfort Zones

Life begins at the end of your comfort zones.

—Neale Donald Welsh,[67]
Author

We are drawn towards those like us. This is a natural human characteristic. We prefer to engage with those with whom we share commonalities. Whether it be a health club, a place of worship, our nationality, our community/neighborhood, our primary language, our ethnicity, our family, our hobbies/passions, our sports, our choices for entertainment, our unit at work, our profession – there are thousands of things that unify us.

There is one common impact of this behavior that can have negative consequences and become a roadblock. I refer to it as the paralysis of "comfort zones." If we aren't careful, we can begin to adopt a habit of only embracing "our people" or community. This can lead to shutting out those different from our network and create barriers between people. We create comfort zone bubbles where we only associate with our tight circle and, often without realizing it, our world becomes a closed community. An unintended result is that we stop adapting, stop engaging with those beyond the bubble, and become closed minded.

Workplace bullies use comfort zones to single out their targets. They capitalize on the target's comfort zones by highlighting their uniqueness, their limited exposure to others, pointing out their ignorance, making fun of their community and driving a wedge to isolate them from their coworkers. If you are unable to reach beyond your comfort zone and make allies with outsiders, you will find it nearly impossible to address a workplace bully.

I encourage all of us to take time to assess our comfort zones – just being aware that we have them can prevent us from myopia. Openly embrace that we are creatures of habit and generally reluctant to venture beyond our comfort zones. At the same time though, be willing to acknowledge that comfort zones can make us afraid or ignorant of others.

Assuming that most of us aren't fond of fear or ignorance, I believe that each of us is responsible to take action towards self-improvement. I have found success by starting with setting realistic goals to give us the confidence and tools to bring us out of our comfort zones.

For example, we can set goals to actively engage with others outside our community, using those at work as perfect starting points. Our coworkers will almost inevitably not all be within our comfort zone. Nor will we be in theirs. Thus, we start from a place of equality. Since we need to build strong working relationships with our coworkers and they have the same goal, it is natural to use this opportunity.

For example, Agnieska confided that her comfort zone was her Polish community. She grew up surrounded by this community, worked in mainly Polish companies, and was anxious to step beyond it. When she started working for a large technology company with a highly diverse workforce, she realized that she had a great deal of learning to do. She initially felt terribly isolated and vulnerable, afraid her lack of diversity intelligence would be uncovered.

Through a series of steady small steps, she began to interact with her coworkers. By asking open-ended questions about their backgrounds and lives, Agnieska slowly developed relationships and built confidence. She developed tools to address her fears of the "unknown others," and her risk averseness to the awkwardness of meeting new and different people. Over months, she overcame her fear of rejection and change. She also confronted her own biases and prejudices. She found herself becoming more open and embracing of others. Personal growth is often difficult but as Agnieska discovered, there was an enormous and fascinating world beyond her Polish comfort zone.

The lesson learned in Agnieska's success is that if we are willing to commit to working on expanding beyond our comfort zone, we become better coworkers, more likely to succeed and more worldly. I encourage you to turn your comfort zone into an acknowledgement of who you are most comfortable with rather than a roadblock to your personal growth.

All of these roadblocks compound upon each other, resulting in our leaders, bosses, or coworkers being unable to take action to assist in dealing with a workplace bully. Everyone faces these roadblocks in one form or another. I believe that we owe it to ourselves, our families, our organizations, and our societies to commit to working hard at self-improvement to break these impasses.

c) An Understanding of the Consequences of Silence

What's the point of having a voice if you're going to be silent when you shouldn't be.

—Angie Thomas,[68]
Author

The third building block for your action plan to address a workplace bully is a deep understanding of the impact of silence. One of the most common challenges when faced with a workplace bully is the overwhelming fear to speak out, even to trusted coworkers. You may fear losing your job, being disciplined, demoted, or replaced by someone willing to act unquestionably. You may fear that those above with authority won't take kindly to a whistle blower. These fears are real – you will be afraid of retribution, of making the problem worse, of not knowing how to speak up. However, it is that silence and fostering the fear of speaking out that enables bullies to thrive. I hope to disrupt our hard-wired tendency toward paralysis and speechlessness by presenting silence through a lens of accountability.

Another common theme for silence that I've heard many times is the idea that ethical decision-making is the sole responsibility of senior management. They have the authority and power to make and implement the decisions, so they are the only ones accountable for taking action. In other words, it's "not my job."

I respectfully disagree. First, each of us owes a duty to ourselves, our organizations, our coworkers, and our families to act with integrity and demonstrate courage in the face of injustice. We have our moral compasses that guide us to be ethical, honest, and professional. Second, as an employee, you have committed to comply with your organization's policies, whatever they may be. Those policies create a positive obligation on all employees to act. Doing nothing is a breach of your policy commitments.

When we are impacted by bad behavior at work, we have two options: action or silence. We can make any decision that we wish, but we're accountable for and must live with the consequences of our decision; every action, including silence, is a decision.

If we choose silence we are accountable for our role in consenting to the bullying. Silence is deemed approval. We may think that saying nothing keeps us safe, avoiding involvement in the conflict. However, that is far from the case. Our silence represents our decision and our position on the matter. When the bullying continues or gets worse (which it will) and we do nothing, we are accountable to ourselves and our colleagues.

There's nothing more humbling than looking in the mirror and taking ownership for your silence. You won't feel right and your moral compass will be screaming to change courses. Another unexpected consequence of silence is that you may find your coworkers rightfully accusing you of enabling the behavior. More serious, your organization may hold you accountable for breaching your workplace respect policy that commits all employees to report bullying when they see it. In effect, silence could detrimentally impact your reputation and your job security.

Silence may also hurt others, leaving them even more vulnerable and empowering the bully to escalate their workplace terrorism. Bluntly put – our silence is selfish. We may be harming the people we want to help. Put yourself in the shoes of the target of the bully for a minute. How would you feel if none of your coworkers spoke out or tried to take action to stop the problem? No servant leader would choose this path. I understand that there are risks and consequences from speaking out. It shouldn't be done blindly – that's why there's an action plan in the next chapter for everyone to ensure that when we do speak out, we're doing it strategically.

Silence also blocks the potential for starting a movement within our team and organization to address the behavior. It is a certainty that our observations and conclusions are shared by others. They may also be afraid to speak out. The first person who shows courage often inspires others to do the same. Think of the recent #MeToo movement as one example of how initiating speaking out led to a global movement to do the same. There is power in numbers and by speaking out, we motivate others to voice their opinions as well.

As a strong believer in self-accountability, it's important that I emphasize that if we've worked through our action plan and decided not to speak out (for good reasons or for the time-being), we have to own our silence. What I mean is that we can't gossip, complain, hint there's an issue, or explode one day because our silence is eating us alive. In essence, we have to "let it go," managing the emotions that come with silence (guilt, anger, resentment, frustration, powerlessness, fear, self-loathing).

To conclude, silence isn't golden. It's a decision with potentially terrible personal and organizational impacts. You'll need to live with yourself, knowing that you're accountable for giving the bully permission to continue on his or her path of interpersonal destruction. You'll also need to live with the risk that you've broken your organization's policy and have acted unethically. Are you prepared to live with those consequences?

d) A willingness to have "fierce conversations"

Our work, our relationships, and our lives succeed or fail one conversation at a time. While no single conversation is guaranteed to transform a company, a relationship, or a life, any single conversation can.

—Susan Scott [69]

The fourth building block for our action plan to address a workplace bully is a commitment to engage in difficult and often confrontational conversations. I refer to these as "fierce conversations." It is a simple fact that, on a daily basis, life presents us with the need to have challenging conversations. Some are easier than others – convincing our colleagues to support our proposal or explaining to our kids why they can't eat ice cream for dinner. In the business world of normal workplace conflict, performance management, dealing with different perspectives and cultures, and addressing workplace disrespect, hard conversations are both necessary and the hallmark of effective relationships and leadership.

We will really be tested when the situation requires a truly fierce conversation – dealing with sexual harassment, racism, bullying, or discrimination at work. No sane person looks forward to these difficult conversations. They will be complex, risky, and volatile discussions that require a carefully considered action plan. However, despite these challenges, we must rise to the occasion, conquer our fears, and have fierce conversations. These conversations make a difference to our self-respect, our relationships, and to results, to workplace culture, and to eliminating the bad behavior.

There are many books on the topics of how to effectively have difficult conversations or resolve conflicts. I consider this a separate topic and suggest that you turn to experts in these areas for help. One book that I recommend is *The HardTalk Handbook* by Dawn Metcalfe. Metcalfe uses a very practical approach to mastering the art of difficult conversations, teaching the reader "the skills you need to succeed at the conversations that make all the difference."[70]

e) A Sound Self-Accountability Framework

It's not only for what we do that we are held responsible, but also for what we do not do.

—Moliere[71]

The fifth and final building block for our action plan to address a workplace bully is a sound personal accountability framework. I've already mentioned that we are accountable for our action or inaction; each is a decision that has consequences. In my experience, one of the reasons that bullying and workplace disrespect continues unabated is that we are rarely willing to accept this responsibility, leading to long-term negative consequences for our self-image, our reputation, our workplaces, and our career success.

At the most basic level, we are paid at work to make good decisions and valuable contributions to our organizations. It is those good decisions that drive innovation, positive behavior, and organizational results. Good decisions in relation to workplace bullying can be transformative for our health and well-being, and that of our coworkers and for our workplace culture.

Yet, time and time again, I have been told stories about good people shirking the responsibility to make these good decisions when it relates to the worst behaviors at work. We are happy to stand up and speak our truth about the strategy for a project but we run for the hills if we are faced with speaking out against workplace disrespect. This has to change. We have to take true ownership of our contributions to our workplace culture and happiness. We have to own the need for candor, compassion, honesty, and courage. We have to face our fears and get involved. We have to make the good decisions we are paid to make.

It is only with an unwavering commitment to get involved that we will conquer the problem. If you aren't prepared to hold yourself accountable for taking action (using a well thought-out action plan) or for your inaction, then I suggest you stop reading this book and take a hard look in the mirror – figure out what's preventing you from voicing your concerns.

***

This chapter has focused on ensuring that you have the building blocks necessary to create a solid foundation for your action plan to address a workplace bully. Regardless of where you work, your job title, or your relationship to the bully, every person will be more successful in bully management if they ensure they have a well-built behavioral foundation. There are many roadblocks that prevent good people from getting involved. If you're ready to make a change, to confront your roadblocks, then you're already building a sound foundation for your anti-bullying action plan.

14

Confronting Disrespect When it Starts

Disrespect is the weapon of the weak.

—Alice Miller[72]

This chapter focuses on how we can effectively respond to the full spectrum of disrespectful behavior. In the case of less severe forms of disrespect (i.e., being interrupted at a meeting, an inappropriate remark, a breach of a boundary, etc.), by taking fair and direct action, when it's appropriate, we not only stop the bad behavior but also lay the groundwork for the possibility of rebuilding the relationship so that we can move past the regrettable offense. This is also possible for many daily workplace conflicts.

Unfortunately, bullying is behavior that falls at the extreme end of the disrespect spectrum. Like harassment, discrimination, and workplace violence, our intervention goal will likely not include the chance to rebuild a relationship. Our main goal is to take action that effectively stops the behavior.

When to Take Action

Action is the foundational key to all success.

—Pablo Picasso[73]

One of the most common questions I'm asked is "*when should I take action against a bully?*" My consistent response to this question is that we stand the best chance of stopping bullying in its tracks if we take action as soon as possible and when it is appropriate – preferably, quickly after the first time the disrespectful behavior occurs.

I make the same recommendation for addressing other forms of bad behavior and conflicts in general at work (or in our personal lives). Any time we encounter behavior on the disrespect spectrum, the most successful tool for stopping it is taking direct action as soon as possible and if it's appropriate. I will discuss the issue of whether your engagement is appropriate later in the chapter. In this section, I focus on the timing of the intervention.

Bullies usually test their potential targets before they decide to fully engage. It is worth a reminder that a bully's actions are deliberate, repetitive, and always disrespectful. Since their actions are intentional, they are usually planned in advance. Bullies are adept observers and careful to initiate. Rarely will a bully begin her assault campaign with a bold move. Rather, her disrespectful behavior usually starts off with a subtle inappropriate remark or passive-aggressive email.

That initial action is designed to test our mettle, our suitability as a target. If we quickly and directly defend ourselves, in many cases, the bully will back off. Like most predators, bullies are risk averse and carefully assess as they go. If their proposed victim has a decisive counter attack that shows strength and confidence, they often disengage, in many cases permanently. By having a tactful, strong, and clear conversation, as early as possible after the initial act of disrespect, we stand the best chance of nipping the behavior in the bud and preventing escalation. Seeing you as a formidable opponent, this conversation may also motivate the bully to leave you alone.

Unfortunately, as discussed in the previous chapter, many of us aren't well prepared for that essential quick defensive response. If we don't have the proper tools and our roadblocks in check, we will be unable to effectively take action the moment that disrespectful behavior occurs at work, including bullying. Sadly, this leaves us ill-equipped to stop the bully in his tracks from the beginning. We miss that golden opportunity that rarely presents itself more than once or twice. All the more reason for us to develop our bully awareness and prevention tool kit now.

Where to Take Action

If we wait for the moment when everything, absolutely everything, is ready, we shall never begin.

—Ivan Turgenev[74]

We now know when to take action – the most impactful moment to respond to disrespectful behavior is the first time it happens. The second component of taking action is to determine where the best place is for this fierce conversation. Conversations, and in the case of email, communications that address an act of disrespectful behavior are most effective if done as soon as possible after the event but under appropriate conditions. The most appropriate conditions are in a private room with a face-to-face conversation.

For example, if Laura is in a meeting with her coworkers and Cecilia rolls her eyes whenever she speaks, Laura shouldn't confront Cecilia in the meeting in front of everyone. Calling out a colleague in a group setting is rarely effective and can easily appear to be a form of public humiliation. The last thing that Laura should do is respond to Cecelia's disrespectful action by being disrespectful herself. Public confrontation also often ignites a spark of gossip that will quickly wind its way throughout your unit and organization.

Instead, Laura's challenging conversation is best done face-to-face, in private, and after a "cooling off" period. Laura's emotions will be running high both during and after the meeting. We are never at our best when we speak from a place of anger and hurt. Thus, I strongly recommend that Laura speak with Cecelia after she has had time to settle her emotions, plan her response, and find a time for a private in-person conversation. Ideally, this is the same day or within the first twenty-four hours after the incident.

There is no replacement for a face-to-face interaction – direct conversations play a powerful role in quickly resolving the issue. With Laura in front of her, Cecelia can't escape from both her bad behavior and the element of humanity – she can see the hurt in Laura's face. The impact of Laura's approach is powerful. She can look Cecelia in the eyes and hold her accountable for the offense she caused. In many cases, the matter will be resolved in a single short conversation and both people can move past the event and rebuild their working relationship. Thus, as intimidating or difficult as it may be, having this fierce conversation is, without doubt, the best course of action.

However, in our complex workplaces, it may not always be possible for the parties to meet in person. In that circumstance, the next best approach is via a video conference or computer meeting using one of the many applications that include live video feed. It's less effective than a physical face-to-face meeting but it's still very impactful to see each other's faces and reactions.

If a computer conversation isn't possible, the next best

option is via the telephone. It's a far less effective means to address disrespectful behavior but it still provides for a live conversation. Hearing a colleague's voice is better than no voice at all.

Finally, there is the least advisable option of using email. Without any personal engagement and with email being so easy to misinterpret, I strongly suggest that email be avoided. In the stories I've heard, email has usually worsened the problem, escalating the emotions, and creating a tit-for-tat battle. Bullies are also highly skilled communicators in the language of subterfuge, deflection, and threats. Email offers them an opportunity to permanently document their defense and usually sparks them into a full bully campaign.

Is it Appropriate to Take Action?

It has long since come to my attention that people of accomplishment rarely sat back and let things happen to them. They went out and happened to things.

—Elinor Smith[75]

We began this chapter with a discussion about when and where each of us can take action to confront disrespectful behavior, including workplace bullying. However, this discussion was premised with one condition – that you only do so if you are comfortable and it's appropriate. In using the word "comfortable," I'm not suggesting that you are only ready to address bad behavior if you relish and enjoy these fierce conversations. No sane person would ever feel that way. Instead "comfortable" and "appropriate" are used as an important reminder that there may be instances when you aren't in the proper place to take unilateral action or the circumstances aren't suitable for you to even try.

For example, if the disrespectful behavior amounts to a sexual assault, involves violence or a threat to your safety, clearly you shouldn't try to address the problem on your own. These are extreme examples but, sadly, there are workplaces that are so toxic that these potentially criminal actions occur. For example, many women have come forth to accuse men in their workplaces of sexual harassment or assault and criminal charges have been laid against them.

We've seen an abundance of media reports recently that shed light on the high-profile cases involving major corporations, entertainment figures, media moguls, governments, police departments, universities, technology titans, and even world leaders. As these cases demonstrate, extreme forms of workplace disrespect can happen anywhere. They also showcase clearly that there are circumstances when victims of workplace disrespect shouldn't take action against the offenders themselves – they need to seek help from others, including the police, legal counsel, and medical professionals.

There are other less extreme situations where it may still be inappropriate to take unilateral action, or the risks involved require that you involve others. For example, if the offender is a person with a high level of power and is known to abuse such authority, it may be best to consider a multilayered action plan that engages others to assist. Alternatively, you may be dealing with a very well-known workplace bully that is entrenched and supported by the senior management.

Before launching into any unilateral action, make sure that you assess the facts carefully. If you realize the situation isn't suitable for taking direct action, then you are better served by devising a long-term anti-bullying action plan (discussed in Chapter 15) that you implement.

How to Take Action

The key to success is action, and the essential in action is perseverance.

—Sun Yet Sen[76]

We've covered both the "when" and "where" of taking action when disrespect happens. From here forward, I'm assuming that you've also determined that it is appropriate for you to take direct action. The inevitable follow-up question is "*How do I take that very first action?*" There is no simple answer to give, so my best response is that "it depends" – on the circumstances, on your organizational policies, on your communication skills, on the people involved, on your place/ role in the organization, and on many other relevant factors. Each fact pattern requires careful assessment to determine what exactly to do and say and whether you need the help of others. However, there are some useful basic guidelines that I believe apply to all situations where you've determined that you're well placed to take direct action, providing a place from which to begin your response planning.

The best way to communicate with a disrespectful colleague is to craft an approach that incorporates the following six components – I call this the "BIFFSE Approach":

1. Be Brief

Outline the problem without embellishment, grand detail, or emotion. Focus on the event of disrespect and your expectation that it never happen again.

2. Be Informative

State with clarity what happened, how it was disrespectful, and that you won't tolerate the behavior. Stay away from describing your feelings and focus on the facts. Maintain a position of strength and emotional control.

3. Be Fair

Don't ask for an unreasonable request or threaten bold action if you don't get what you want. Remember, we are humans and we make mistakes, including your badly behaved colleague. Give the offender a chance to reply and listen. He may have a sincere reason for his behavior (such as he was having a terrible day and his behavior was an unfortunate by-product) or he may immediately apologize. That is the best result you could hope for – a clarification of his motive and an authentic apology. However, if he goes into defense, denial, or attack mode, quickly restate your concern and stand your ground. You may have to agree to disagree and move directly into stating that, despite his defense, you expect the offensive behavior to stop.

4. Be Firm

Your colleague must understand that you've drawn a line in the sand and that you will not accept anything but a cessation of the bad behavior. Once this is done, end the conversation by thanking him for meeting with you and that you look forward to moving past this regrettable event.

5. Be Silent

This is a short conversation and afterwards you need to refrain from gossiping or re-hashing it. You've done your job of informing your colleague what happened and what you expect in the future – now let it go and give the other person a chance to improve. Your hope is to rebuild the relationship with your colleague. By staying silent, you place the responsibility for behavioral improvement squarely on your colleague's shoulders and show emotional maturity. Be patient and, if you see an improvement, by all means, express appreciation for the positive change.

6. **Email follow up**

This is a critical component of the conversation. Always follow up with a sincere thank you email. Reinforce that you are grateful your colleague met with you. More importantly, summarize the event in a sentence or two and restate that you are holding your colleague accountable to an improved behavioral standard. This email serves as a permanent record of the event and your expectation. If there is another incident, you can refer back to this email and, with even stronger language, repeat the first conversation with all the same steps. You've also documented the event for your human resources department, supervisor, or your colleague's supervisor should you need to seek their help. In the worst-case scenario, you've secured some very helpful evidence that your lawyer can use to demonstrate when the behavior began and that you took direct action to prevent it from reoccurring.

I appreciate that without any context, the BIFFSE process I've just described is challenging to put into practice. To reinforce this process, I've created a fact pattern and conversation that will hopefully provide clarity so that you can take your own action when disrespect first occurs. The fact pattern is based on a story that was shared with me at a conference where I was a presenter. I crafted the fictitious conversation as a practical tool to assist in learning how to put the BIFFSE process into our daily work lives (and personal lives).

Fact Pattern

Sayyid and Yiwen work together in healthcare at a hospital. They are coworkers in the same unit responsible for diagnostic testing of patients. Yiwen had an innovative idea to improve the testing process for their MRI system. She discussed it with Sayyid in a series of emails.

In a meeting with their unit's team and their manager, the team discussed challenges meeting their goals and Sayyid raised Yiwen's idea as a possible process improvement. He gave no credit to Yiwen for the idea and acted as if it was entirely his own. When Yiwen tried to speak at the meeting, Sayyid interrupted her, preventing her from speaking up and clarifying that the process improvement was her idea.

Yiwen was naturally very upset and legitimately felt that Sayyid had "stolen her idea." Yiwen was hurt and betrayed. She knew she had to directly confront Sayyid. Using the BIFFSE approach, below is the strategy and the conversation she had with Sayyid:

Place
Yiwen organized a meeting with Sayyid the following morning in a meeting room they often use in their unit.

Mental status
Yiwen spent time after the event bringing her emotions under control. She went for a walk after the meeting, avoided Sayyid for the remainder of the day, discussed her feelings with a trusted mentor that evening and ensured that she had calmed down and was thinking clearly. She planned her approach with a clear mind.

Conversation
Yiwen's discussion points include all the elements of the BIFFSE model. After each important discussion point, I clarify which aspect of the BIFFSE model is applicable.

> Yiwen: "Good morning Sayyid. Thank you for meeting with me today. I want to talk with you about the team meeting yesterday."

(Brief – Yiwen immediately focuses on the issue at hand).

> "At the meeting when we discussed the issue of saving time in the MRI testing unit, you told everyone about my idea. You know that this was my idea as I shared it with you in emails (which

> *she has copies of in front of her). You also wouldn't let me speak or clarify that this was my idea. This was disrespectful and unfair. It also doesn't align with our workplace respect policy."*

(Informative – providing clear background without getting into too many details).

> *"I want you to send an email to our team clarifying this matter and apologize for forgetting that I originally came up with this idea."*

(Fair and Firm – note Yiwen isn't asking that he apologize for stealing her idea or for not letting her speak. She is allowing Sayyid an opportunity to resolve the problem and save face. But she is very clear about what she expects from Sayyid. Also note that Yiwen says nothing about how she felt – she focused on the behavior and that it was disrespectful).

Yiwen pauses to give Sayyid a chance to respond. fully prepared for a variety of responses. Fortunately, Sayyid responds in the best possible way.

> *Sayyid: "I'm so sorry – I totally forgot that it was you that first raised this concept. It's been quite a few weeks that we've been hashing out the concept between us and I failed to remember it's your idea. I didn't intend to offend you or to be rude in the meeting. I got excited when management liked the idea and understand that I took over the discussion. I will send an email to everyone right away."*
>
> *Yiwen: "Thank you – I really appreciate that. I hope this never happens again."*

(Firm – she reinforces the expectation for both the present and the future).

> *Yiwen: "That's all I wanted to speak with you about. Thanks again for meeting with me."*

(Silent – Yiwen doesn't continue discussing the issue, her feelings, or any other issue. She limits the discussion to the single problem and promptly leaves the meeting room).

Yiwen gets back to her desk. Later in the morning after a reasonable time has passed she sends Sayyid an email as follows:

> *Hi Sayyid. Thank you again for meeting with me today about the team meeting yesterday. I appreciate that you acknowledged that the idea for the MRI unit's innovation came from me originally. Thank you for also agreeing to clarify this matter with the team and for agreeing this won't happen again.*
>
> *Yiwen*

(Email Follow Up – Yiwen's email reinforces both the content of the meeting's discussion and the result. She focuses on the next step that Sayyid agreed to take and that this behavior won't be tolerated going forward).

This example hopefully illustrates that applying the BIFFSE process to our workplace challenges isn't difficult. The conversation will likely be stressful but it will be effective. Your coworker will have no illusions about where you stand. It takes practice but, over time, I assure you that it works. The first time you are faced with a real life BIFFSE situation, I recommend that you take the time to plan and write out your proposed conversation, much like in the above example.

I further recommend that you plan for a variety of responses from your disrespectful coworker. As we discuss in the next section, we may not get the matter resolved with only one conversation. In order to be as well-prepared as possible, plan for that possibility. For example, consider the possibility that Sayyid could totally deny that the idea was Yiwen's. He could also aggressively defend his actions, accusing Yiwen of lying. Each possible response can be handled using the BIFFSE approach. You may not get the matter resolved or the response you hoped for; however, you will have taken action and made it clear what your position and expectations are going forward. Even if you agree to disagree, you can clarify that you remain firmly of the opinion that you've been treated disrespectfully.

What if it Doesn't Work the First Time?

Perseverance is not a long race, it is many short races one after the other.

—Walter Elliot[77]

How many times must we remind our children not to chew with their mouths open? I use this as a reality check – in many cases, the disrespectful behavior that caused offence may take time to eliminate. Given our human fallibility and that our patterns are difficult to change, it often takes more than one reminder or event of disrespect before the behavior begins to measurably improve.

Thus, we need to be prepared to have more than one fierce conversation with our colleague. I recommend using the same approach in each subsequent conversation but with more emphasis on accountability and the consequences for failing to stop. Refer back to the previous conversation and remind your colleague that this has already been discussed. Ask what is driving them to continue to behave badly.

In my experience, these subsequent discussions become easier, in the sense that you've laid a very clear path for accountability. Continue on the path and amp up the risk of failure. For example, after a couple of reminders, you may feel it's appropriate to warn your colleague that you'll have to speak to their supervisor or human resources if things don't improve.

I've also discovered in quite a few cases that there are more facts and information that are shared in the follow-up conversations. For example, Ricardo continued to show intolerance and impatience with Logan, a younger colleague, despite a number of interventions from Logan. In a moment of frustration, Ricardo shared that he wasn't on his best behavior and was exhausted because he was caring for an unwell elderly parent. Ricardo acknowledged his behavior was unacceptable but provided some background as to why he was so easily frustrated and volatile.

Ricardo's life challenge doesn't excuse him from accountability for his disrespectful actions – he still has to work harder to behave respectfully. However, it provides an explanation for what's motivating him. This new information may give rise to an opportunity for a different approach. Logan now understands that Ricardo isn't intentionally being disrespectful. Logan can change the conversation to show empathy and compassion by expressing genuine concern for his family situation. With almost no effort, Logan and Ricardo's relationship can shift from a place of conflict to one of collaboration.

For example, Logan could suggest that Ricardo speak with human resources about options for him to take some time off for elder care leave. Alternatively, there may be an employee assistance program that Logan can suggest that Ricardo could contact to obtain resources to help him with counselling or find professional help to assist with the care of his sick parent. Logan may also need to speak with his supervisor as he may not be best placed to follow up on this matter. Logan's empathy opens the door to mutual understanding which, in many cases, results in the end of the disrespectful behavior.

Unlike the example with Logan and Ricardo, if there isn't any new information that comes forward, then I recommend that you continue on the path of fierce conversations.

After each conversation, it's essential to continue to send follow-up emails. They are critical proof that document what happened and provide a post-mortem, analyzing what you have learned. Don't hesitate to change course, revise your accountability plan, and to continue to press the need for change. Also, I don't recommend that you have more than a few interventions. If your colleague is repeatedly ignoring your request and the disrespect isn't going away, you may need to get help from others.

Do you need help from others?

You are never strong enough that you don't need help.

—Cesar Chavez[78]

I'm frequently asked about when we should get others involved in dealing with a workplace respect problem, including our colleagues, supervisors, and human resources personnel. While each situation has to be analyzed on its own merits, it's important to assess the benefits and risks of choosing to seek the help of others. I have assessed the pros and cons of asking for help from a variety of "others" separately.

Also, in Chapter 15, I discuss the possibility of engaging others to help you in crafting and implementing your anti-workplace bullying action plan. The material in this chapter may be helpful and relevant to whether you choose to seek the help of others in your personal action plan.

Seeking Help from Your Coworkers

Humble people ask for help.

—Joyce Meyer[79]

When seeking the help of others, it's important to understand how they might be of assistance and what is their sphere of influence. Your coworkers are best seen as potential emotional supporters and sideline allies. They may seem like the most logical people for you to turn to for help – they understand your workplace, they see the dynamics created by the bully, they may have witnessed you being disrespected, they may even be your friends or trusted confidants. However, care should be taken before you share your situation with them or ask them for help.

First, remember that your coworkers rarely, if ever, are in a position to help – they have the same authority as you do. They don't have the power to make the decisions that need to be made. They are often feeling vulnerable, afraid, and uncomfortable too. From the many stories that I've been told, it is quite common that, in the face of disrespectful behavior, coworkers are usually concerned about their own well-being and reluctant to help or get involved. Most say their motivation is driven by a legitimate concern that if they help, they are putting themselves at risk for being bullied and disrespected too. Consequently, fear paralyzes them from helping or makes them ineffective most of the time.

Secondly, despite the sensitivity of the situation, coworkers naturally tend to gossip with others. While they sincerely think they are helping (i.e. by warning others or trying to build support for you), gossip is never helpful. It spreads like wildfire and before you can blink, everyone, including the disrespectful person or bully, has heard about your "problem."

Furthermore, thanks to the gossip chain, the story has likely taken on a life of its own with many embellished "facts" or new features that never were part of the situation. You've lost control of the process and information, usually rendering your proposed first intervention ineffective. In fact, it has often escalated, making the problem worse.

At the initial intervention phase, my recommendation is to only involve your coworkers for a limited purpose, if at all. For example, if you know that coworkers witnessed the first event of disrespect, you may wish to mention them in your documentation, keeping track of the details of the event. You also may want to speak with them to clarify that they saw or heard the same thing you did in order to ensure that you didn't misinterpret the event. That is the extent to which they may be helpful to you at this point. I don't recommend getting into a discussion about your emotions, what you plan to do next, or asking for them to do anything.

It is with this limited purpose that I recommend you consult with your coworkers. If the matter doesn't resolve after the first intervention or if you need to move into crafting your anti-bullying action plan, they may play a more important role. Otherwise, I suggest you keep the matter to yourself at this early stage, avoiding the risks of sharing it with them.

Seeking Help from Your Manager

You don't have to do it all by yourself.

—Elizabeth Dehn[80]

Your supervisor/manager has a role that involves competing responsibilities and priorities. In general, your manager has a primary duty to enforce your organization's behavioral standards and to support you and manage your work and performance. Managers also owe a duty to protect you if you're being disrespected by a colleague. Thus, she normally should be an ally that you can rely on if you can't resolve the issue yourself or you're uncomfortable trying to. This is particularly true if your manager is an engaged servant leader who stands behind her staff.

However, your manager owes the same duties to everyone else she manages, including the disrespectful person (if he works in your unit). This can create roadblocks to success when you seek her help. Depending on the parties involved, your manager's multi-layered duties may create barriers to her effectiveness at dealing with your disrespectful colleague. For example, if the misbehaved colleague is another person that she manages, you can appreciate that this is a more complicated situation. She has to ensure that she is fair, striking a careful balance and following relevant dispute resolution policies.

What if the person being disrespectful is another manager? Again, your supervisor will have a different challenge to address given that it's one of her colleagues that she works with at the management table. Even more complex is the situation where your supervisor or a senior executive is the problem. It bears reminding that more than half of the time, your bully is your manager. This doesn't necessarily mean that you should never speak with your supervisor. On the contrary – she may be willing to listen and be prepared to assist (or accept responsibility for her own bad behavior).

However, there are risks involved with seeking her help and, therefore, I recommend that you assess various issues beforehand. While each situation is unique and will raise its own considerations, there are some baseline questions for certain situations that I suggest you investigate prior to taking any action to engage your manager (my list of questions isn't exhaustive).

Each question is likely to raise others – that is normal and reinforces why it's important to step back and evaluate the pros and cons of involving your supervisor. Also, I haven't covered all the permutations of relationships that your supervisor could have with the offending colleague. My intention is to increase your awareness of the potential range of issues to consider so that you can focus on those that are most relevant to your situation.

I've separated the baseline questions into the most common fact patterns that you may face. Also, you'll notice, many of the questions are the same or similar for each situation. The purpose of this exercise is to ensure that you carefully assess the appropriateness of asking your manager for help, using the questions as a tool for ensuring you've developed the right strategy for your next step in dealing with your disrespectful coworker.

Situation 1

If the disrespectful coworker is from another unit that your supervisor doesn't manage:

- Is your supervisor a hands-on, engaged leader that is willing to address conflict and supportive of a respectful workplace?

- What is your relationship like with your supervisor? Do you trust him? Do you feel he is effective? Does he have your back?

- Historically what is your supervisor's relationship with your coworker, if any?

- Has your coworker had a pattern of problem behavior before with others? (You may not know but you can investigate.)

- Has your coworker been disciplined for disrespect in the past? (You may not know.)

- How long has your supervisor been in her role?

- What is your supervisor's relationship with your coworker's supervisor?

- What is your supervisor's relationship with human resources?

- How have your workplace respect policies been enforced in the past?

Situation 2

If the disrespectful coworker is also a person that your supervisor manages:

- Historically what is your supervisor's relationship with your teammate?

- Has your teammate had a pattern of problem behavior before with others? (You may not know but you can investigate.)

- Has your teammate been disciplined for disrespect in the past? (You may not know.)

- How long has your supervisor been in her role?

- How well does she know each of you?

- How have your workplace respect policies been enforced in the past?

- Do you trust your supervisor to be fair to your both?

- What is your supervisor's relationship with human resources?

Situation 3

If the disrespectful person is another supervisor:

- Historically what is your supervisor's relationship with the other supervisor and with his boss? What is your supervisor's relationship with her boss? What is the power balance between each of them and all of them as a whole?

- Realistically, would your supervisor take on her colleague at the management level and hold him accountable? Would her boss do the same? (She may need help from senior management.)

- Has the disrespectful supervisor had a pattern of problem behavior before with others? (You may not know but you can investigate.)

- Is the disrespectful supervisor "untouchable" (i.e. does he weld significant power and has historically been supported, regardless of his behavior)?

- Has the executive disciplined other managers for disrespect in the past? (You may not know.)

- How long has your supervisor and the offending supervisor been in their roles?

- How have your workplace respect policies been enforced in the past?

- What is your supervisor's relationship with human resources?

- Has HR historically been supportive of your supervisor, or what have they done in the past when a manager breaches organizational respect or ethics policies?

Situation 4

If the disrespectful person is your supervisor:

- Historically what is your supervisor's relationship with the executive and with his boss? What is the power balance between them?

- Realistically, would your supervisor's boss take on your supervisor and hold him accountable?

- Has your supervisor had a pattern of problem behavior before with others (you may not know but you can investigate)?

- Is your supervisor "untouchable" (i.e., does he weld significant power and has historically been supported, regardless of his behavior)?

- Has the executive disciplined other managers for disrespect in the past? (You may not know.)

- How long has your supervisor been in his role?

- How have your workplace respect policies been enforced in the past?

- What is your supervisor's relationship with human resources?

- Has HR historically been supportive of your supervisor or what have they done in the past when a manager breaches organizational respect or ethics policies?

Situation 5

If the disrespectful person is someone above your supervisor (i.e. a more senior executive, a director, a vice-president, or the president/CEO) whom I collectively refer to as an "executive":

- Historically what is your supervisor's relationship with the executive? What is the power balance between them?
- Who is the executive's boss? What is your supervisor's relationship with him? What is the power balance between them?
- Realistically, would the executive's boss take on the problem and hold him accountable?
- Has the executive had a pattern of problem behavior before with others? (You may not know but you can investigate.)
- Is the executive "untouchable" (i.e. does she/he weld significant power and has historically been supported, regardless of her/his behavior)?
- Has senior management or the board of directors (if applicable) disciplined other executives for disrespect in the past? (You may not know.)
- How long has the executive been in his role?
- How have your workplace respect policies been enforced in the past?
- What is the executive's relationship with human resources?
- Has HR historically been supportive of the executive, or what have they done in the past when a executive breaches organizational respect or ethics policies?

By taking time to evaluate the pros and cons of whether you should seek the assistance of your supervisor, I believe you'll ensure that your path forward is well-informed and more likely to succeed. Sober second thought is always better than a knee jerk reaction. Involving your manager may be a great option or ill advised – each situation must be assessed on its own merits and facts. By using these questions as a risk assessment tool, I believe you'll know what to do and, more importantly, what to avoid.

Seeking Help from Human Resources

I am convinced that nothing we do is more important than hiring and developing people. At the end of the day you bet on people, not on strategies.

—Lawrence Bossidy[81]

As discussed in Chapter 11, human resources has a very unique role and, as a result, is not always the appropriate place to turn to for help. Sometimes you have no choice but to go to HR, but I believe we must do so with an understanding of their role and the limits of their capacity to take action to deal with the disrespectful coworker.

I have a great deal of respect and empathy for HR professionals. I've worked closely with many of them and have learned that they walk a tightrope on a regular basis, balancing the needs of their organizations, the executives, the political landscape, business pressures, and the welfare of the employees. Human resource professionals have a challenging role that involves competing responsibilities and priorities.

As supported by the quote above from Lawrence Bossidy, they have the organization's best interests as their top priority. Their job is to ensure that strategic decisions related to the human resources (all employees) support the vision and goals of the organization. They also have a different risk lens than others. As a starting point, they are concerned about the rights and welfare of the employees. They must enforce their own policies, relevant laws, and take action to address allegations of poor performance, ethical breaches, and unacceptable behavior. But, their risk lens is much wider, particularly when faced with a high-risk situation like workplace bullying, harassment, or violence. When the stakes are high, they must also consider legal risks, financial risks, public relations risks, reputational risks, and business risks.

On the one hand, HR staff are empowered to enforce all organization policies (including workplace respect policies, codes of ethics, hiring/discipline/firing protocols). On the other hand, they are looking for the best solution for the organization and trying to protect the business – and not necessarily the individual. That is why we repeatedly see our organizations resolve high-risk bullying, sexual harassment, or discrimination matters through legal settlements that quietly pay victims to depart (with hush money), and keep the person that caused the mess employed.

Look no further than CBS, Viacom, Ford Motor Company, Bank of America, the Royal Canadian Mounted Police, a host of politicians, including the President of the United States, and other high-profile global organizations for the most recent egregious examples of how perceived risks for the organization trumped the lives of victims and remaining employees. HR is sitting at the table when these decisions are made. But they are one voice of many.

In the world of risk management and business, the best strategy may not ultimately protect the victim. These "solutions" are often viewed as a cost of doing business or, more simply, as the best risk management strategy in the circumstances. In hindsight, we've seen some of these so-called "strategic" short-term decisions become long-term organizational nightmares that can be so catastrophic they bring the organization to its knees, as in the case of the Weinstein Company.

This makes for a very tricky landscape when it comes to badly behaved employees, particularly in relation to bullying.

The landscape becomes more like a minefield when the person that is behaving badly is a senior employee, an executive, or someone with significant influence. HR generally has its eyes on the ground and they usually see what is really going on. It's rare that HR doesn't know there is a bully or disrespectful person at work, particularly when that person wields power and authority.

They may want to take action against the problem but we can see why things aren't straightforward. Their perspective may be overruled by broader organizational or political interests. In effect, despite their best intentions, they may be denied the chance to address the problem or have no authority to do so. Further, when they try to take action, the organizational policies aren't helpful and lack adequate processes to ensure the matter is handled fairly and impartially.

Finally, it is common that HR professionals don't have the specialized training to make them effective at handling highly complex and sensitive matters like workplace bullying. The result is that they may fail to take action or the action they take isn't helpful and, unintentionally, they contribute to the problem.

I've tried to provide insight into the risks of seeking help from HR to take action against a first-time event of disrespect. By taking time to evaluate the pros and cons of whether you should involve human resources personnel, I believe you'll ensure that your path forward is well-informed and more likely to succeed. We will also discuss involving HR in Chapter 15 in the context of crafting our anti-bullying action plans.

***

As with other conflict, the best results in quashing bullies and bad behavior are usually achieved when we directly and strategically engage, as early as possible, to resolve the problem. However, care must be taken to plan our approach and evaluate whether we need to involve others in order to be effective. If we follow a process and stick to the goal, there is a good chance we'll prevent further disrespect if we confront it right away. By taking time to assess the situation, the risks, and the pros/cons of asking others to help us, I believe that we will make sound decisions and improve our chances of success.

15

Anti-bullying Action Plans for Individuals

A goal without an action plan is a dream.
—Nathaniel Branden[82]

If you've had those first direct conversations to try to resolve the disrespectful behavior problem but it's clear who you're dealing with is a bully that isn't interested in changing their behavior, then it's time for a deeper dive, crafting an action plan for dealing with the bully. Each of us will need a unique personal anti-bullying action plan that takes our particular workplace and circumstances into consideration.

Depending on who you are and where you fit in your organization, there may be unique options for action available to you. For example, executives, by virtue of their senior leadership roles, potentially have more capacity to take direct action than a lower-level employee. Likewise, a unionized employee has options that aren't available to a non-unionized person. Finally, those directly targeted by a bully clearly need a much different action plan than a colleague witnessing the abuse but are out of range of the bully's target zone.

Each action plan below is designed to assist persons in specific roles or relationships vis-á-vis the bully.

1. A Senior Executive Anti-bullying Action Plan

You have enemies? Good. That means you've stood up for something, sometime in your life.

—Winston Churchill,
Former Prime Minister of the United Kingdom[83]

For those in the executive ranks, use your influence and authority to make change. You have many strong arguments to convince those who challenge change. It won't be easy, but your organization has put you in a leadership role for a reason. Leadership may sometimes feel lonely and difficult – do the right thing anyway. As we heard from Desmond Tutu, "neutrality isn't an option."

Your action plan incorporates leading your organization to implement the above-mentioned organizational anti-bullying action plan. It also incorporates the plan below for managers in terms of demonstrating your own commitment to respectful workplace culture. In addition, there are some actions that you can take to leverage your authority and motivate positive change towards a bully-free zone at work.

Get informed

In order to appear credible, it's important to have the knowledge and capacity to speak with authority. As noted earlier, there is a plethora of information about workplace bullying available. There are also experts available with whom you can consult.

Not only must you be fully informed about bullying, but also about the benefits of a bully-free workplace. Further, when planning for change, it's helpful to have a deep awareness of your organizational culture and historical reality. Identify your allies and the change-intolerant. Appreciate the hurdles that you and the organization will need to overcome.

Get a plan

As with all organizational change initiatives, there is no replacement for a well laid-out business plan and strategy. Identify and consult with all stakeholders. Begin conversations with your cheerleaders to plant the seeds for change. Demonstrate proof of the return on investment (ROI). Seek the assistance of subject matter experts. Engage with HR. Perhaps you need assistance from experts external to your organization who can guide you to a practical, realistic strategy for achieving success. Devise a plan and courageously move it forward.

Engage others with influence

Within every organization there are people in positions with significant political influence and decision-making authority. Like all successful strategies, you will need their support. They may very well become the sponsors of the program. It's equally important to know who the foes are. Develop a strategy for addressing their concerns and for the possibility that they will openly oppose the anti-bullying initiative. The more you appreciate change management strategies, the better prepared you will be when the naysayers try to derail your strategy.

Use examples from other organizations

For many executives and senior managers, the motivation for change is derived from a desire to keep up with or gain advantages against the competition. They also are focused on their own reputation and opportunities. By using very persuasive and factual examples from other organizations rather than anecdotal references, you will earn credibility points.

If you can turn the dialogue into a "what's in it for me" discussion, focusing on how an anti-bullying program advances the agendas of both the organization and the executives, buy-in is more likely. Instead of a focus on what it costs to implement change, perhaps it will be more effective to focus on what it will cost if they do nothing. Lost opportunity cost and ROI (return on investment) is language that executives relate to.

Incorporate change management into your plan

It is naïve to expect that workplace culture change is easy to implement. Critical to all project plans is the incorporation of sound change management practices. The test of success isn't whether your organization has implemented an anti-bullying program – it is whether it is working, embraced, and effective. There are many tactics for ensuring high levels of adoption and for testing levels of acceptance when implementing change. From effective and continuous training to performance metrics that measure success, incorporate change management strategies in the plan.

Be courageous and unwavering

There will be people who will try to roadblock your work. Known bullies in your organization will immediately begin to work against your initiative, using their supporters in the executive ranks. Expect arguments that focus on the program being a waste of time and money, unnecessary (because bullying isn't a problem), without merit compared to other organizational priorities, etc. Stay steadfast and firm in your commitment. Leadership isn't about popularity – it is about doing what is right and inspiring change.

***

As a senior executive, you have the influence and authority to activate change. It won't be easy or quick, but your change leadership could permanently alter the course of your organization. It will undoubtedly shape your destiny as a leader. Be strategic and use your network of power brokers. Devise a plan and be courageous. A bully-free workplace will serve you and everyone in your organization, paying dividends far beyond your expectations.

2. A Manager/Unit Leader Action Plan

It is better to lead from behind and to put others in front, especially when you celebrate victory when nice things occur. You take the front line when there is danger. Then people will appreciate your leadership.

—Nelson Mandela[84]

There are many things managers can do to confront bullying, even if your organization has yet to implement an anti-bullying strategy. It begins with you and your leadership style. By setting your personal code of conduct and ensuring that everyone you lead with aligns their performance and behavior, you can have significant positive impact.

It can take constant vigilance to keep the workplace respectful and free from bullying. Managers can use several strategies to keep their own behavior in check and to foster civility among others. They include the following:

Keep yourself in check

Managers set the tone and create the standards for behavior. Be aware of your actions and consider how you come across to your team and in your workplace. If you eye roll when you are frustrated or lose your patience, you effectively communicate to your team that they are free to act the same. Disrespect and prepare to be disrespected back.

Be a behavioral role model

In a survey, the Workplace Bullying Institute found that:

> *25% of managers who admitted to having behaved badly said they were uncivil because their leaders—their own role models—were rude. If employees see that those who have climbed the corporate ladder tolerate or embrace bullying behaviour, they're likely to follow suit. So turn off*

> *your iPhone during meetings, pay attention to*
> *questions, and follow up on promise.*[85]

Solicit others' feedback

It is healthy and an empowering leadership tool to seek reality checks from the people who work with or for you. Such feedback can prove very insightful and helpful. It also shows you are interested in learning and improving. You can't expect your team to learn from you if you aren't willing to do the same.

As a manager, it is important to create an environment where staff are encouraged to speak up. At a minimum, seek regular feedback in safe and confidential ways from your team. Ensure any survey or 360-degree review process includes questions about your leadership style, the level of respect and value that staff feel, and what you could do to improve.

Teach respect

It's amazing how many managers don't understand what it means to be respectful. In one *Harvard Business Journal* survey it was found that "one quarter of ill-mannered managers surveyed said that they didn't recognize their behavior as disrespectful."[86]

This sounds hard to believe yet it is true. It isn't helpful to condone rudeness by arguing that society has lost all awareness of basic manners and politeness. Do you want to be a leader or a follower? Do what you can to teach respect.

Create rules for group engagement

Even without a workplace respect policy, as a manager, establishing team rules for behavior can have an impact on your team. It can also enhance their performance, team engagement, and job satisfaction. Why not begin a conversation with your team about the kinds of behavior they expect from each other? By getting your staff involved, they are more likely to embrace whatever ground rules for respect they have helped create. It can be as simple as agreeing that no one interrupts when another is speaking, arriving on time, and shutting off devices during meetings. It seems trite or obvious yet so many managers miss this opportunity.

Performance manage

Performance management is an important component for a respectful work environment. As so aptly noted by Christine Porath and Christine Pearson in a 2013 article in the *Harvard Business Journal* [87]:

> *Collegiality should be a consideration in every performance review, but many companies think only about outcomes and tend to overlook damaging behaviors. What behavior does your review system motivate? All too often we see organizations badly miss the mark. They want collaboration, but you'd never know it from their evaluation forms, which focus entirely on individual assessment, without a single measure of teamwork, attitude, or respectfulness."*

If you can, revise the performance metrics to include behavioral components that enhance workplace culture. This creates a culture of accountability and positive reinforcement. If you don't have that authority, lobby for change. In the meantime, it takes little effort to recognize and thank people who behave well, even if your organization isn't ready to put behavioral metrics in the performance strategy.

On the flip side, it is equally important to address bad behavior from the moment it starts. Drawing lines in the sand is essential, even if it feels confrontational or uncomfortable. How can you expect people to improve if you're not ready to have that hard conversation with them about their disrespectful behavior? As a manager, it is your responsibility to lead. That includes courageously addressing bad behavior quickly and assertively.

Organizations often avoid taking action, though, and most incidents go unreported, partly because employees know nothing will come of a report. Set your own course and show that you expect more from your team. If you want to foster respect, take complaints seriously and follow up.

***

A warning to those who think consistent workplace respect is an extravagance: Just one habitually offensive employee critically positioned in your organization can cost you dearly in sickness costs, lost employees, diminished performance, lost customers, and lost productivity. It can also cost you your own job and reputation as an effective manager.

3. An Action Plan for Targets of Bullies

A hero is an ordinary individual who finds the strength to persevere and endure in spite of overwhelming obstacles.

—Christopher Reeve[88]

If you are a target of a workplace bully, it's reassuring to know that there are many things you can do to protect yourself and create a plan for coping. Having a plan provides much comfort, alleviating the sense of helplessness, solitude, and fear that targets face. It gives you a sense of focus and purpose aside from simply surviving another day at work.

The target's action plan contains two separate sections. The first is a discussion of what positive actions targets can take. The second contains overarching considerations that help targets ensure they maintain perspective.

Targets can use several strategies to both cope and address the bully at work. They include the following:

Stay healthy

There are many health risks associated with bullying. Constantly check in with yourself to ensure your health is stable. Without your health, nothing else matters. The risk is real.

Develop strategies for ensuring you are taking care of yourself (i.e. regular doctor visits, heart-to-heart conversations with trusted advisors and family, exercise/stress-reduction programs). It is very easy to lose sight of the health impacts that bullying is inflicting upon you. You may need to take sick leave or vacation time to protect your health, or take breaks. Make them a part of your plan. Don't waiver or feel this represents weakness. In fact, it represents you taking back power.

Educate yourself

It is essential to understand what bullying is and how it is carried out in order to move forward. Step 1 in the education process is to get informed. Knowledge is indeed power. Often targets lack a deep awareness of the impact and genesis of bullying. Do some research to ensure you understand what is behind bullying, why you have been targeted, what you've been through, what your feelings are, etc. This will not only demystify the bullying experience, it will help align your expectations, goals, and action plan with reality. If you're reading this book, you're well on your way in terms of education.

Step 2 of the education process is doing your investigative homework. Find out all of the pieces of the bullying puzzle before you even try to figure out what to do. Some of the most important pieces of the puzzle include the following:

- Whether there are policies in place related to workplace behavior (and what they contain);
- What training, if any, has been provided or is available relating to workplace respect;
- Whether there is legislation that might impact the situation (i.e. anti-bullying, human rights, etc.)
- Whether there is a formalized complaints process for employees and, if so, whether it is fair, safe, and effective;
- Whether others have complained and, if so, what was the result;
- What is the general workplace culture and the history of how issues related to disrespectful behavior have been handled;
- Whether HR is well-trained or have handled a bullying scenario before;
- How long the bully has been employed and what influence she/he has;
- The engagement level of senior management and whether they actually care or are aware enough to respond;
- Whether you have any close allies (coworkers or influencers) willing and unafraid to assist; and
- Any other relevant aspect of your workplace bully and culture that you think is important.

Document everything you learn (but not on your work computer). The more detailed and the more objective, the better. This process will both focus you away from feeling victimized and ensure that whatever strategy you create, it aligns with your workplace reality and appropriately sets your expectations.

Do a self-check

With all the information in hand, do a self-check and consider whether you might be misinterpreting the behavior, overreacting to it, or whether you've unknowingly contributed to the problem. I know from experience that some of my engagement contributed to the bullying problem. By losing our frustration, acting out, fighting back at the wrong time, baiting the bully, or other unchecked responses, we may not be doing ourselves any favors.

Do your best work

While you complete your investigation and devise your plan, do your best work. Try to maintain your integrity and professionalism. Easy to say but hard to do when you're in such a toxic and difficult situation. Try not to sabotage yourself or the bully and don't create additional performance issues for the bully to jump on. Sometimes there may be ways for you to devise some tactics in order to avoid, placate, or ignore the bully. For example, it may help to stroke the aggressor's ego. Even a small gesture, such as ending an email with "Thanks so much for your help" or complimenting the person on something, can help. Without being sycophantic, give it a try and see if it has an impact.

Don't blame yourself

It is almost a given that you will assume the problem and situation is your fault when it's not. The bully chose you based on her/his warped perception of the world and what is a threat. It's normal to think that you must be doing something wrong for someone to treat you this way at work. Given the fact that you are likely one of the most competent and diligent employees, it's equally understandable that your response is to try to fix the situation by working harder and proving your worth.

Remember to step back and appreciate that the bully is acting aggressively because he feels threatened by you. This has little to do with the work or you, and everything to do with the bully's messed-up mind.

Stand up for yourself

I appreciate that much of what you can do depends on the workplace and local culture. Nonetheless, bullies are known to step back if the target defends himself. Don't be afraid to call out the bad behavior when it happens. I believe very strongly in making immediate corrections. If the bully says something inappropriate (i.e., calling you "stupid" or something condescending like "honey"), respond right away if it's appropriate: "I don't like being called that. Please use my name."

If it's inappropriate or you're uncomfortable with an immediate response, use the BIFFSE process as described in Chapter 14 as soon as you're able. After the meeting or instance of name calling, you could say, "I didn't like being called 'Honey.' It is disrespectful and contrary to our workplace respect policy." Show that there is no reward for treating you that way. The message should be: "Don't mess with me; it won't be worth your effort."

This line drawing is useful because it may lead to an opportunity to try to solve it informally. Bullies aren't fools (far from it) – they might reassess the situation and back away. This is especially possible if you take serious note that you have a bully in your midst and assess what you might be able to do to reduce the bully's perception that you are threatening. Act accordingly and it may result in a détente of sorts.

Establish a support network

Regardless of your plan, it is important to have sounding boards who are reliable and supportive. In the beginning, it is recommended that these people be outside of your work. Gossiping or sharing your frustrations with a work colleague is likely unhelpful.

Instead, there are trusted mentors, friends, and wise

people to turn to. It is important to have a place to vent, to seek feedback, to strategize, and to simply have a shoulder to lean on. Building a support network that can help get you through the tough times makes a significant difference. Also, as hard as it may be, share your feelings openly and without sugarcoating. Those who want to help you can only do their best work if you are honest about the depth and breadth of the problem.

Get counseling (if possible)

Many organizations have Employee Assistance Programs that are confidential – use them! If you have the means, get a counselor who specializes in workplace bullying (sadly there are plenty of them). The guidance of trained professionals is a tremendous help to coping and making sure you stay balanced. Being proud won't serve you. You don't have all the tools but others do.

Get a plan

This is the most important step in your strategy. There is simply no replacement for good planning and a clear breakdown of what you need to do. Treat this like a project and create a business plan with all the essential elements. Often the planning process provides a much-needed sense of purpose and focuses work life away from the bully.

Define your goals. This could mean that you are going to create and implement an exit strategy. It could mean you want to gather all the information needed to launch a formal complaint. Regardless, it's important to know what your plan is focused on achieving and what you need to do to get the desired result.

Once you have your goals in place, you'll need to gather information. Outline each task, with a plan for how to obtain the data and a realistic time frame within which to get it. Similar to project management, you also have to determine your scope. How far do you need to go to ensure you have everything, and what are the limits of the plan?

Risk manage as best you can and always try to stay nimble. The bully will continue to operate while you are implementing your plan. Consequently, be ready to adjust and even scrap your plan if necessary.

Also, it is important to identify the stakeholders and assess their impact on your plan. Whether it is HR, your coworkers, other managers, an influential executive, or the bully, each person plays a role in the plan. Thus, your plan should consider how to manage each stakeholder and how he or she helps your plan succeed.

Like any strategy, there are some elements that help drive the likelihood of success. They include the following:

Develop an exit strategy.

Regardless of what you hope to achieve, make certain you are also working on an exit strategy. It is possible that the best strategy is to develop your organizational exit plan. It may get so bad that you have to pull the trigger on leaving the job. It's helpful to consider many options for exiting. There are more than you might think.

Some of the obvious exit strategies include quitting, finding a new job (within or outside your current organization), or transferring to another department. There are others, though, such as taking an educational leave, taking sick/ stress leave (this requires doctor support), or hiring a lawyer to intervene on your behalf (i.e., to negotiate a severance package or even launch legal action).

One factor worth mentioning is that targets are prone to let their ego get in the way of healthy and self-preserving decision-making. The Workplace Bullying Institute has done online surveys that show more targets stay in a bullying situation because of pride (40%

of respondents) than because of economics (38%).[89] Rather than worrying about letting the bully win, you're better off focusing on your own well-being.

Regardless of what it contains, an exit strategy is essential to protect yourself if things become impossible or your health is being impacted. You may not be able to change this toxic workplace but you can leave a message about why you left and move onto a harmonious workplace. Insist on an exit interview and even then, write a letter to your CEO telling her why you left the organization using as much objective information as possible.

The bottom line is that even if you want to take action against the bully, don't suffer unnecessarily. If the situation persists and you can leave, do it. Try to plan ahead and if you can find a new job while you're still in the toxic one, even better.

Document. Investigate. Secure objective proof.
Aligning these tasks with your action plan goals, the documentation and investigation process is a critical component for success. If your plan is to launch a formal bullying complaint, consider what information would be needed to create the most impactful and effective strategy to present a complaint. How would you obtain this evidence?

Document every incidence of unacceptable behavior but focus on facts you can prove and secure the irrefutable evidence to do it. If there were others who witnessed an event write that down, along with the date, time, place, and explanation of the situation. This is a stealthy challenge and you'll need to be patient, careful, and smart. Just like solving a major crime, you're pulling all the pieces of evidence together to present the most persuasive case possible. Don't put anything on your work computer. Ever.

Know your organization's limitations.

Even if you are clearly being bullied, the chances of change or success in many organizations are low. There is hope with new laws and improved awareness but accept reality. Appreciate the organizational landscape and align your expectations accordingly. Despite even the best arguments or an airtight case, it's sometimes hard for organizations to take action. I've discussed all the reasons why our organizations fail us as targets – this helps keep perspective on the chances of success. If you're in an abusive situation at work, the most tenable solution may be to leave — if that's a possibility.

Control what you can.

The only aspect of bullying that you can control is how you respond. As hard as that is to accept, the sooner you can come to terms with your very limited sphere of influence, the more likely your action plan will be realistic.

Don't expect you can control others; particularly those you are hoping are your allies. Even if your coworkers feel terrible about what they are witnessing, they are afraid too. They don't want to become the target. They may not have your back.

Also, before you approach anyone from within, assess the risks and the likely response options. My advice to targets is to appreciate the reality and role of HR: They have the organization's interests paramount. They are assessing the extent of the company's liability. This is especially true if the bully is a member of management. HR is rarely an ally and often makes the situation worse.

Expect realistic reactions from HR, your supervisor, and senior management. Your investigation will provide you with baseline information to help gauge what to expect.

Be courageous but calculated.

Be strategic, focused, and patient. Only move ahead when you are ready. Where you can, call out the inappropriate behavior in the moment. Be prepared for conflict and challenges. Realistically assess the risks and challenges you would face if you raised the flag. Be courageous but sensible.

Enlist help, but choose very carefully.

Consider whether you have any colleagues willing to join forces with you – there is power and credibility in numbers. Given that targets are commonly the most respected and well-liked employees, it is likely that you have alliances at work — peers and people above and below, who can be your advocates and champions. When you're ready, talk to those supporters and see what they can do to help, whether it's simply confirming your perspective or speaking on your behalf.

Focus on costs and impacts.

If your plan is to present a complaint, it helps to stay as far away from the personal as possible when making a pitch for action. Even though you have been deeply hurt and personally impacted, don't tell a story of emotional wounds. Make an argument that the bully is costing the organization money and show how. Demonstrate as objectively as possible that harboring the bully is impacting organizational success.

You may want to point to some well-known examples to compare (i.e., recent bad press for Amazon's "Darwinian culture"). When you have someone's ear, focus the conversation on how the bully's behavior is hurting the workplace. Talk about how it's affecting morale and performance. If people have left, are on sick leave, or projects are failing, these facts are very helpful. Personal pleas rarely work and too often degenerate into "he said-she said" type arguments.

***

A focused, practical, and realistic plan is fundamental to coping with a workplace bully. The goal of the plan may vary but the requirement for a plan is universal. The best way to cope with a workplace terrorist is through a clear strategy that considers all the options and prioritizes the means to achieve the goals of the plan. Taking control of what you can and empowering yourself to deal effectively with the bully will help you avoid making many mistakes and losing sight of your vision.

4. An Action Plan for Coworkers, Witnesses, and Bystanders

You gain strength, courage, and confidence by every experience in which you really stop to look fear in the face. You are able to say to yourself, "I lived through this horror. I can take the next thing that comes along."

—Eleanor Roosevelt[90]

If you are a coworker of a target or a witness from another unit, it's reassuring to know that there are many things you can do to help the target, protect yourself, and create your own plan for coping. To think that coworkers aren't deeply impacted by the bullying is naïve and counter-intuitive. Coworkers suffer many of the target's feelings of anxiety, fear, and stress – work becomes a place of daily struggle, vulnerability, and pain.

Educate yourself about bullying and how those around the organization might respond. Devising your own plan provides much comfort, and alleviates the sense of helplessness, guilt, and fear that witnesses face. It gives you a sense of focus and purpose aside from simply surviving another day at work.

An important point for coworkers is that your plan should consider many of the same factors that form part of the coping strategies for targets. Consequently, your plan must reflect the reality of your workplace, what you can control, what you can do to protect yourself, and how you might be able to assist the target. Every action plan requires a tailor-made strategy.

There are many similarities between a target's action plan and that of a witness but viewed through a different lens. The best advice for coping for coworkers is to create an action plan that incorporates the following:

Stay healthy

There are many health risks associated with bullying suffered by coworkers and bystanders. Watching a friend or colleague being broken down by a campaign of interpersonal destruction is no different than witnessing a violent crime. There are emotional and physical reactions that are natural and can negatively affect you. Constantly check in with yourself to ensure your health is stable.

Develop strategies for ensuring you are taking care of yourself (i.e., regular doctor visits, heart-to-heart conversations with trusted advisors and family, exercise/stress-reduction programs).

Educate yourself

Just like for targets, Step 1 in the education process is to get informed. Often witnesses lack a deep awareness of the impact and genesis of bullying. This leads to a sense of utter helplessness because you don't comprehend the chaos.

Do some research so that you understand why your colleague has been targeted, and what you're feeling. This will not only demystify the bullying experience, it will help you understand the mix of emotions you are experiencing. For example, it helps to appreciate that it is normal to feel fear each day at work – fear for what may happen to the target, fear that you may become a target, fear of uncertainty, and other fears. It further comforts when you learn that witnesses commonly feel "witness paralysis," which leads to feelings of guilt because you have done nothing to either help the target or confront the bully. With helpful information you will be better able to align your expectations, goals, and action plan with reality.

Do your best work

In an effort to avoid becoming a target while you complete your investigation and devise your plan, do your best work. Try to maintain your integrity and professionalism. Try not to act out emotionally, alerting the bully to the fact you sense something bad is going on. Don't create any performance issues for the bully to jump on. Do your best to stay away from the bully and modify your behavior where appropriate.

Document everything

Regardless of what you ultimately choose to do, it is essential to document every incidence of unacceptable behavior. Focus on facts and securing irrefutable evidence to support your version of the events.

Not only might your documentation help the target in the event of an investigation or formal complaint, it may also help you feel like you are positively contributing to the effort to eliminate the bully. Pull all the pieces of evidence together to present the most persuasive case possible. Prepare as if you were going to be interviewed by a bullying complaint investigator.

Provide support for others

Knowing that you are neither a counselor nor a trained HR staff member, try to do what you can to provide support both to the target and your coworkers. You're all going through an unpleasant time and it helps to feel you are sharing the burden.

Consider what the target is trying to manage and how you might provide emotional support or other compassionate assistance. Sometimes just listening is enough. Help the target reason things out and make sound decisions given the realities of your workplace.

If called upon or there is a chance, volunteer to be interviewed in the event of a formal complaint and investigation. This is your chance to actively contribute to eliminating bullying and to use the evidence that you carefully acquired. This might take courage and be very uncomfortable but remember the words of Martin Luther King – "The time is always right to do what is right."

Consider a team response

There is truth about the adage of "strength in numbers." This is especially the case regarding bullying. Organizations really wake up when a team raises the flag in a coordinated and well laid-out strategy. Even a few coworkers banding together can have a significant influence. Like targets, if you are going to consider this approach, it is essential to get a plan and work together to implement it. All of the components of the target's action plan should form part of your plan.

If a team response isn't possible, perhaps some coworkers will at least provide support by signing a letter to the executive. There are different ways to lend a hand without being the spokesperson.

Finally, if you decide that you want to lodge your own formal complaint or make a personal plea to an influential executive, it is even more important to get a plan.

Get a plan

With all of the noted plan components to consider, formulate your goals and strategic approach. Focus on identifying the objective negative impacts that the bully is creating for the team and target. The more that you can emphasize the costs, the more likely you will reach your influential empathetic leader.

***

Coworkers, witnesses, and bystanders can play a change leadership role in helping address bullying in the workplace. There is no doubt that such engagement will be difficult and unpleasant. Try to focus on how it will feel to have taken a risk, helped make a difference, and proven the value of integrity, compassion, and team orientation. Perhaps think of the message that it sends to everyone else in the unit, others in your organization, your children, and your friends. Goodness begins in the mirror.

Conclusion

Our greatest weakness lies in giving up. The most certain way to succeed is always to try just one more time.

—Thomas A. Edison[91]

Every workplace seems to have a bully on staff. Workplace bullying is incredibly prevalent and organizations face challenges in effectively addressing or eliminating it. In addition, the impacts of bullying are severe, costly, and felt throughout the organization and even beyond.

For far too long, we have expected our organizations to wake up and take the initiative to address this global epidemic. The facts are irrefutable and the impacts obvious – how could our organizations not deal with such a clear and costly problem? In my opinion, we've placed too much faith that our leaders had the tools, motivation, and awareness to remove this preventable toxin that ruins workplace culture. While it makes sense that we should look to our leaders to address bullying, we don't need to look far to see that approach isn't working.

I believe the only way that the status quo can change is if enough of us decide to take action. As a society, we need to disrupt the system that supports and, all too often, protects the bullies and harassers. In effect, we need to take the leadership reins and start a global workplace bullying awareness campaign and action plan.

I'm well aware that we won't change the world instantly, but like the #MeToo movement, we can progress far beyond a hashtag. As each of us learn skills to take action and put those skills into action, the impact reverberates beyond us, representing the "disruption movement" that I believe is necessary for change. Each of us has the choice to either be part of the movement for change (and accountable for taking action) or to remain aligned with the status quo.

The good news is that increased global organizational and public awareness, recent research, and expanding illegalization of workplace bullying are having positive impacts. Employers around the world are becoming more informed of the impacts and costs associated with bullying. They are seeing more objective data and examples to learn from. The opportunity cost of failing to take action is beginning to resonate for organizations.

While it may seem like the higher goals of doing what is ethical, moral, or responsible matter less, I think that what matters most is that the world is waking up. If the only way that organizations will respond to bullying is by being fed the business case for eliminating bullying, then we should all provide our organizations with the diet of numbers and statistics that will motivate action.

It is a simple fact that if we demonstrate to our employers and senior executives that taking initiative in addressing bullying early on, much larger financial, ethical, legal, human resource, and project problems will be avoided. Eventually, our initiatives will lead to wider support for zero tolerance for bullying in the workplace regardless of circumstance, societal norm, or jurisdiction.

For all of us impacted by bullying, there is much to learn and to do to become part of the movement forward to change. There are action plans and steps that we can take regardless of where we live, where we work, what role we have, and what workplace culture we face. They will be different depending on many factors, but what is important is that we have information and tools to engage effectively.

It is my sincere hope that with this handbook, readers feel less afraid, better informed, and properly empowered to courageously address workplace bullying. With that higher purpose and hope for the future, I find inspiration from those who continue to press for change and each of you I speak with at events, workshops, webinars and online. Keep the faith – change is coming. Martin Luther King Jr. said "the time is always right to do what is right."

It's time.

Endnotes

1. Michael M. Honda, BrainyQuote.com (retrieved October 27, 2015, http://www.brainyquote.com/quotes/quotes/m/michaelmh519241.html).

2. Clive Boddy, "Bullying and Corporate Psychopaths at Work" (December 3, 2012, available from https://www.youtube.com/watch?v=tlB1pFwGhA4&index-=19&list=PLlszBLRhOFq8MTEunsB1psfl_c4EUyyTk).

3. Martin Luther King, Jr., BrainyQuote.com (retrieved October 27, 2015, http://www.brainyquote.com/quotes/quotes/m/martinluth106169.html).

4. Patricia G. Barnes, Surviving Bullies, Queen Bees and Psychopaths (United States: Patricia G. Barnes, 2012; updated July 2013).

5. Jim Kouzes & Barry Posner, The Leadership Challenge (San Francisco, CA: Jossey-Bass, 2008).

6. Kofi Annan, BrainyQuote.com (retrieved October 27, 2015, http://www.brainyquote.com/quotes/quotes/k/kofi-annan389917.html).

7. Workplace bullying, 2015, Merriam-webster.com (accessed October 15, 2015, from http://www.merriam-webster.com/dictionary/workplacebullying).

8. Ståle Einarsen, Bullying and Emotional Abuse in the Workplace: International Perspectives in Research and Practice (Taylor & Francis: 2003).

9. The WBI Definition of "Workplace Bullying" (accessed July 24, 2015; available from http://www.workplacebullying.org/individuals/problem/definition/).

10. "The Definition of Workplace Violence". (accessed October 10, 2015; available from https://www.osha.gov/SLTC/workplaceviolence/).

11. The Devil Wears Prada (accessed on October 25, 2015; available from https://en.wikipedia.org/wiki/The_Devil_Wears_Prada_(film)).

12. Antoine de Saint-Exupery, BrainyQuote.com (retrieved October 27, 2015, http://www.brainyquote.com/quotes/quotes/a/antoinedes137412.html).

13. Margaret Heffernan, BrainyQuote.com (retrieved October 27, 2015, http://www.brainyquote.com/quotes/quotes/m/margarethe556959.html).

14. "PMI Ethical Decision-Making Framework, pmi.org (2013, accessed on July 24 2015; available from http://www.pmi.org/About-Us/Ethics/Ethics-Resources.aspx).

15. Tom Felton, BrainyQuote.com (retrieved October 27, 2015, http://www.brainyquote.com/quotes/quotes/t/tomfelton472945.html).

16. Erica Pinsky, Road to Respect: Path to Profit (Canada: 2009), 78.

17. Macklemore, BrainyQuote.com (retrieved October 27, 2015, http://www.brainyquote.com/quotes/quotes/m/macklemore483477.html).

18. Ray Williams, "How Workplace Bullying Harms every Employee in the Toxic Work Environment," The Financial Post, February 21, 2015. (Available from http://business.financialpost.com/executive/management-hr/how-workplace-bullying-harms-every-employee-in-the-toxic-environment).

19. Christine Porath and Christine Pearson, "The Price of Bullying in the Workplace," Harvard Business Review, January 1, 2013 (Available from http://hbr.org/2013/01/the-price-of-bullying/ar/1).

20. Workplace Bullying Institute, workplacebullying.org (available from http://www.workplacebullying.org/wbiresearch/wbi-2014-us-survey/).

21. Jennifer Grasz, "Careerbuilder.com Study Finds More Workers Feeling Bullied in the Workplace," Careerbuilder.com (August 29, 2012; available from http://www.computerweekly.com/news/2240085434/IT-workers-being-bullied-says-union).

22. Clare Rayner, "The Incidence of Workplace Bullying," Journal of Community and Applied Social Psychology, 1997, (Vol. 7 No. 3) pp. 199-208.

23. Ståle Einarsen, "The Nature and Causes of Bullying at Work,"International Journal of Manpower (MCB University Press, 0143-7720: 1999, Vol. 20 No1/2) pp16-27.

24. Rebecca Thomson, "IT Workers Being Bullied, Says Union," Computerweekly.com (March 4, 2008, available from http://www.computerweekly.com/news/2240085434/IT-workers-being-bullied-says-union).

25. Clarence Thomas, BrainyQuote.com (retrieved October 27, 2015, http://www.brainyquote.com/quotes/quotes/c/clarenceth137493.html).

26. "Treasury Board of Canada Policy on Harassment Prevention and Resolution" (accessed on September 20, 2015; available from http://www.tbs-sct.gc.ca/pol/doc-eng.aspx?id=26041&section=text).

27. Stephanie Pappas, "Work Bully Victims Struggle with Dangerous Stress," Livescience.com (January 12, 2012; available from http://www.livescience.com/17872-workplace-bullying-stress.html).

28. Sam Walton, BrainyQuote.com (retrieved October 27, 2015, http://www.brainyquote.com/quotes/quotes/s/samwalton163394.html).

29. Albert Schweitzer, BrainyQuote.com (retrieved October 27, 2015, http://www.brainyquote.com/quotes/quotes/a/albertschw133530.html).

30. Workplace Bullying Institute, www.workplacebullying.org (available from http://www.workplacebullying.org/wbiresearch/wbistudies/).

31. Octavia E. Butler, BrainyQuote.com (retrieved October 27, 2015, http://www.brainyquote.com/quotes/quotes/o/octaviaeb646144.html).

32. Workplace Bullying Institute, workplacebullying.org (available from http://www.workplacebullying.org/wbiresearch/wbistudies/).

33. Herbert Spencer, BrainyQuote.com (retrieved October 27, 2015, from BrainyQuote.com Web site: http://www. brainyquote.com/quotes/quotes/h/herbertspe109568. html).

34. Ståle Einarsen, Bullying and Emotional Abuse in the Workplace: International Perspectives in Research and Practice (Taylor & Francis: 2003).

35. Pappas, Livescience.com.

36. Impact on Health Survey, 2012, Workplace Bullying Institute, worplacebullying.org (available from http://www. workplacebullying.org/2012-d/).

37. Workplace Bullying Institute, worplacebullying.org (available from http://www.workplacebullying.org/wbiresearch/wbistudies/).

38. Ian Erickson, "Bullying in the Workplace A Problem for Employers," Guardian Newspaper, February 1, 2014.

39. Jodi Kantor and David Streitfield, "Inside Amazon: Wrestling Big Ideas in a Bruising Workplace," New York Times, August 16, 2015.

40. Erickson, Guardian Newspaper, February 1, 2014.

41. Dalai Lama, BrainyQuote.com. (retrieved October 27, 2015, http://www.brainyquote.com/quotes/quotes/d/dalailama386167.html).

42. Pinsky, Road to Respect, 63 - 68.

43. Pinsky, Road to Respect, 66.

44. Desmond Tutu, BrainyQuote.com (retrieved October 27, 2015, http://www.brainyquote.com/quotes/quotes/d/desmondtut106145.html).

45. Jack Welch, BrainyQuote.com (retrieved October 27, 2015, http://www.brainyquote.com/quotes/quotes/j/jackwelch173308.html).

46. Benjamin Franklin, BrainyQuote.com (retrieved October 27, 2015, http://www.brainyquote.com/quotes/quotes/b/benjaminfr383794.html).

47. Workplace Bullying Institute, worplacebullying.org (available from http://www.workplacebullying.org/wbire-search/wbi-2014-us-survey/).

48. Peter Drucker, BrainyQuote.com (retrieved November 2, 2015, http://www.brainyquote.com/quotes/quotes/p/peterdruck131069.html).

49. Workplace Bullying Institute, worplacebullying.org (available from http://www.workplacebullying.org/wbi-z-bl-1/).

50. Orrin Woodward, Goodreads.com (retrieved September 18, 2015, https://www.goodreads.com/author/quotes/249881.Orrin_Woodward?page=2).

51. Albert Camus, BrainyQuote.com (retrieved October 27, 2015, http://www.brainyquote.com/quotes/quotes/a/albertcamu118026.html).

52. Mark Graban, Quotes.com (retrieved October 12, 2018, http://www.picturequotes.com/mark-graban-quotes).

53. Greenleaf, R. (1991). The Servant As Leader (Rev. ed.). Indianapolis, IN: Robert K. Greenleaf Center.

54. Kouzes, J. & Posner, B. (2008). The Leadership Challenge. San Francisco, CA: Jossey-Bass.

55. Warren Buffett and Bill Gates, "The Economic Crisis and Ethics" (November 9, 2009, available from https://youtu.be/VTFmUuJlTZY).

56. Sam Walton, BrainyQuote.com (retrieved February 27, 2016, http://www.brainyquote.com/quotes/quotes/s/samwalton163394.html).

57. Ackerman, Dean and Ackerman Anderson, Linda, "How Command and Control as a Change Leadership Style Causes Transformational Change Efforts to Fail" (January 2014, available from http://changeleadersnetwork.com/free-resources/how-command-and-control-as-a-change-leadership-style-causes-transformational-change-efforts-to-fail#sthash.jHB883gX.dpuf).

58. Cooper, Anderson (correspondent), "The King of Coal" (March 6, 2016, CBS 60 Minutes available from http://www.cbsnews.com/news/60-minutes-massey-coal-don-blankenship-king-of-coal/).

59. Jodi Kantor and David Streitfield, "Inside Amazon: Wrestling Big Ideas in a Bruising Workplace," New York Times, August 16, 2015 (Available from http://www.nytimes.com/2015/08/16/technology/inside-amazon-wrestling-big-ideas-in-a-bruising-workplace.html?_r=0).

60. Barry McKenna, "Turing Volkswagen Scandal Show Firms are Willing to Roll the Ethical Dice," The Globe and Mail, Sept. 25, 2015 (Available from http://www.theglobeandmail.com/report-on-business/international-business/turing-volkswagen-cases-show-firms-still-willing-to-roll-ethical-dice/article26549560/).

61. Elliott Brettland, "FBI to probe Sepp Blatter as disgraced FIFA chief finally heads for the exit six days after cash scandal that rocked world football," The Daily Mail Online, June 2, 2015 (Available from http://www.dailymail.co.uk/sport/sportsnews/article-3107842/Sepp-Blatter-resigns-president-FIFA-amid-bribery-scandal.html).

62. Orrin Woodward, Goodreads.com (retrieved February18, 2016 https://www.goodreads.com/author/quotes/249881.Orrin_Woodward?page=2).

63. Woolf, Virginia, Picturequotes.com (retrieved July 8, 2018, http://www.picturequotes.com/without-self-awareness-we-are-as-babies-in-the-cradles-quote-464453).

64. Unknown, Quotavocabulary.com (retrieved July 18, 2018, https://quotabulary.com/quotes-about-negative-attitude).

65. Robbins, Rhonda Louise, Goodreads.com (retrieved August 4, 2018, https://www.goodreads.com/author/show/13850628.Rhonda_Louise_Robbins).

66. Shaw, George Bernard. Brainyquote.com (retrieved on August 6, 2018 https://www.brainyquote.com/quotes/george_bernard_shaw_385438).

67. Welsh, Neale Donald. Brainyquote.com (retrieved on August 6, 2018, https://www.brainyquote.com/quotes/ neale_donald_walsch_452086).

68. Thomas, Angie. The Hate U Give. (Balzer & Bray. 2017. ISBN# 9780062498533)

69. Susan Scott. goodreads.com (retrieved on October 12, 2018, https://www.goodreads.com/work/quotes/16957-fierce-conversations-achieving-success-at-work-and-in-life-one-conversa).

70. Metcalfe, D. (2018). The HardTalk Handbook (United Arab Emirates. ISBN: 978-9948-356-6).

71. Moliere. Wisdomtrek.com (retrieved on June 10, 2018 https://wisdom-trek.com/day-237/moliere-quote-ac-countability/).

72. Miller, Alice. Quotefancy,com (retrieved on August 15, 2018 https://quotefancy.com/alice-miller-quotes).

73. Picasso, Pablo. Entrepreneur.com (retrieved on July 16, 2018 https://www.entrepreneur.com/article/244301).

74. Turgenev, Ivan. Awandervine.com (retrieved on August 16, 2018 http://awanderingvine.com/30-quotes-taking-action/).

75. Smith, Elinor. Awandervine.com (retrieved on August 16, 2018 http://awanderingvine.com/30-quotes-taking-action/).

76. Sen, Sun Yet. Brainyquote.com (retrieved on August 16, 2018, https://www.brainyquote.com/authors/sun_yatsen).

77. Elliot, Walter. Brainyquote.com (retrieved on August 16, 2018, https://www.brainyquote.com/topics/persever-ance).

78. Chavez, Cesar. Burndishedchaos.com (Retrieved on August 16, 2018, https://burnishedchaos.com/quotes-about-asking-for-help/).

79. Meyer, Joyce. Burndishedchaos.com (Retrieved on August 16, 2018, https://burnishedchaos.com/quotes-about-asking-for-help/).

80. Dehn, Elizabeth. Burndishedchaos.com (Retrieved on

August 16, 2018, https://burnishedchaos.com/quotes-about-asking-for-help/).

81. https://www.m3ssolutions.com/article/top-20-motiva-tional-quotes-hr-professionals/199.

82. Branden, Nathaniel. Azquotes.com (Retrieved on August 16, 2018, https://www.azquotes.com/quote/710543).

83. Winston Churchill, BrainyQuote.com (retrieved October 27, 2015, http://www.brainyquote.com/quotes/quotes/w/winstonchu135210.html).

84. Nelson Mandela, BrainyQuote.com (retrieved October 27, 2015, http://www.brainyquote.com/quotes/quotes/n/nelsonmand393048.html).

85. Workplace Bullying Institute, worplacebullying.org (available from http://www.workplacebullying.org/wbiresearch/wbistudies/).

86. Christine Porath and Christine Pearson, "The Price of Bullying in the Workplace."

87. Porath and Pearson. Ibid.

88. Christopher Reeve, BrainyQuote.com (retrieved October 27, 2015, http://www.brainyquote.com/quotes/quotes/c/christophe141891.html).

89. Workplace Bullying Institute, worplacebullying.org (available at http://www.workplacebullying.org/wbiresearch/wbi-2014-us-survey/).

90. Eleanor Roosevelt, BrainyQuote.com (retrieved October 27, 2015, http://www.brainyquote.com/quotes/quotes/e/eleanorroo121157.html).

91. Thomas A. Edison, BrainyQuote.com (retrieved October 27, 2015, http://www.brainyquote.com/quotes/quotes/t/thomasaed149049.html).

Bibliography

Barnes, Patricia G. *Surviving Bullies, Queen Bees and Psychopaths.* United States: Patricia G. Barnes, 2012; updated July 2013.

Boddy, Clive. "Bullying and Corporate Psychopaths at Work" (December 3, 2012, available from https://www.youtube.com/watch?v=tlB1pFwGhA4&index-=19&list=PLlsz-BLRhOFq8MTEunsB1psfl_c4EUyyTk).

Cardemil, Alisha R., Esteban V. Cardemil, and Ellen O'Donnell. "Self-Esteem in Pure Bullies and Bully/Victims: A Longitudinal Analysis." *Journal of Interpersonal Violence* (August 2010, Sage Publications) 25 (8): 1489–1502. doi:10.1177/0886260509354579. PMID 20040706.

Einarsen, Ståle. *Bullying and Emotional Abuse in the Workplace: International Perspectives in Research and Practice.* Taylor & Francis, 2003.

Einarsen, Ståle. "*The Nature and Causes of Bullying at Work*," International Journal of Manpower (MCB University Press , 0143-7720: 1999, Vol. 20 No1/2), pp16-27.

Erickson, Ian. "Bullying in the Workplace: A Problem for Employers," *Guardian Newspaper* (February 1, 2014). http://guardianlv.com/2014/02/bullying-in-workplace-a-problem-for-employers/#jVfFzPGYWtSlXGdq.99.

Habib, Marlene. "Bullies Can Make Workplace Intolerable," *The Globe and Mail* (December 19, 2011. Last updated: September 6, 2012). http://www.theglobeandmail.com/report-on-business/small-business/sb-managing/bullies-can-make-workplace-intolerable/article4201840/

Kantor, Jodi and David Streitfeld. "Inside Amazon: Wrestling Big Ideas in a Bruising Workplace," *The New York Times* (August 16, 2015). http://www.nytimes.com/2015/08/16/technology/inside-amazon-wrestling-big-ideas-in-a-bruising-workplace.html?_r=0.

Kelsey, Lindsay. "The significance of Amazon's work culture — and how the *Times* article may impact the retail giant," Retaildive.com (August 19, 2015). http://www.retaildive.com/news/the-significance-of-amazons-work-culture-and-how-the-times-article-may-i/404192/.

Kouzes, J., and B. Posner. *The Leadership Challenge.* San Francisco, CA: Jossey-Bass, 2008.

Pfeffer, Jeffrey. "3 lessons from the Amazon takedown," *Fortune.com* (August 18, 2015). http://fortune.com/2015/08/18/amazon-new-york-times/.

Pinsky, Erica. *Road to Respect: Path to Profit.* Canada: 2009.

Porath, Chrisine and Christine Pearson. "The Price of Incivility," *The Harvard Business Review* (January 1, 2013). http://hbr.org/2013/01/the-price-of-bullying/ar/1.

Project Management Institute. *PMI Code of Ethics and Professional Conduct* (2006). Accessed August 10 2014. http://www.pmi.org/About-Us/Ethics/Ethics-Resources.aspx.

Project Management Institute. *PMI Ethical Decision-Making Framework* (2013). Accessed July 24 2014. http://www.pmi.org/About-Us/Ethics/Ethics-Resources.aspx.

Rayner, Clare. "The Incidence of Workplace Bullying"(Journal of Community and Applied Social Psychology ,1997, Vol. 7 No. 3), pp. 199-208.

Stephens, Tina and Jane Hallas. Bullying and Sexual Harassment: A Practical Handbook. Elsevier, 2006. p. 94.

The Workplace Bullying Institute website. Accessed July 24 2014. http://www.workplacebullying.org.

Thomas, Angie. The Hate U Give. Balzer & Bray. United States. 2017. ISBN# 9780062498533

Thomson, Rebecca. "IT Workers Being Bullied, Says Union," Computerweekly.com (March 4, 2008, available from http://www.computerweekly.com/news/2240085434/IT-workers-being-bullied-says-union).

Williams, Ray. "How Workplace Bullying Harms every Employee in the Toxic Work Environment," The Financial Post (February 21, 2015). http://business.financialpost.com/executive/management-hr/how-workplace-bullying-harms-every-employee-in-the-toxic-environment.

Paul Pelletier is a corporate lawyer, project manager, international public speaker, and business executive with over 25 years of experience in senior roles in government and industry.

During his career, on more than one occasion, Paul realized he was the target of disrespectful workplace behavior and workplace bullying. He suffered in silence until his health forced him to take a different approach. Leveraging his workplace bullying experiences, he is now an advocate, consultant, and expert in workplace respect, diversity, and bullying. Helping organizations establish strategic policies, programs, and processes for openly, fairly, and effectively addressing disrespectful workplace behavior is his focus. He is a regular presenter at global conferences and other events.

Other books by Paul Pelletier
Workplace Bullying: It's just Bad for Business

www.paulpelletierconsulting.com.

LinkedIn contact:
https://www.linkedin.com/in/paulapelletier/

www.ingramcontent.com/pod-product-compliance
Lightning Source LLC
Chambersburg PA
CBHW060303220326
41598CB00027B/4215